New edition 1990

Limited edition published 1989
Copyright © National Army Museum, London 1989

Edited by Mark Nicholls and Linda Washington

Designed by Alastair Pether and Teresa Sullivan

ISBN 0 901721 17 4

All profits from the sale of this publication will be divided
between the National Army Museum Development Trust Appeal,
and the Dunkirk Memorial Appeal organised by the Royal Naval Association
and the Royal British Legion.

Cover artwork based on an original photograph:
A soldier of the 3rd County of London Yeomanry (Sharpshooters) in Summer 1940,
when the Regiment was employed on Home Defence duties in the United Kingdom.
As an armoured unit the men of the Regiment wore the black beret.
National Army Museum 7503-63-1

Printed by Maidenhead Graphic Printers

'AGAINST ALL ODDS'
THE BRITISH ARMY OF 1939-40

Written by
David Smurthwaite, Mark Nicholls, and Linda Washington
with guest authors

CONTENTS

'AGAINST ALL ODDS'

'Different' and 'original' are two adjectives which it is hoped may be applied with some degree of fairness to this Publication, produced to accompany a Special Exhibition mounted in the National Army Museum entitled **'Against All Odds!': The British Army of 1939-40** 'Different' because we are concerned with the British Army exclusively in the early stages of the Second World War, when Neville Chamberlain was Prime Minister, and final victory far from certain. 'Original' because much of the material is published in this Volume for the first time, especially photographs, objects, and archival material from the Collections of the National Army Museum.

In summary, the staff of the National Army Museum have examined afresh the nature of the British Army which mobilized to face the Nazi threat; that Army which spent a bitter winter waiting both at home and in France for an assault that was long-delayed, and which fought in Norway and France during the disastrous campaigning of Spring 1940. The personnel of that Army, their equipment, training, and deployment on a worldwide stage - for initially the World War was fought by an Empire in alliance with an Empire, the British with the French - all came under scrutiny in displays which drew not only upon the Museum's own collections but also upon the generous support of the Institutions listed below.

Of necessity, the story stretched both backwards and forwards in time; back to the problems of re-equipping and expanding a neglected Army which confronted British Governments of the 1930s, and forward to the grim days of June 1940 when France succumbed to invasion and the BEF - or a part of it - came home. It was, maybe, 'Against All Odds' that 'a very well and fully equipped Army', in Churchill's

words, was made ready to take up its positions in France by October 1939. In the aftermath of that experience, the Army faced perhaps the highest odds that it has ever known.

It is one advantage of fiftieth anniversaries that many of those who survived the events commemorated are still very much alive and can speak for themselves, authoritatively and vividly, upon the subject. This Volume - designed both to serve as handbook and as an informative tribute to the men who served in that Army - draws not only upon the written and photographic sources of twentieth-century history, published and unpublished, but also upon those same recollections. It is hoped that it will stir still more memories, and give those who did not live through those days a sense at least of what it meant to serve in the British Army through the first year of the War.

Running from 7 October 1989 to 10 June 1990, the Special Exhibition was devised by a Project Team led by Linda Washington, aided by Andrew Robertshaw and Martin Hinchcliffe, and supervised by David Smurthwaite. Invaluable assistance and research was provided by Mark Nicholls, Marion Harding, Peter Boyden, Lesley Smurthwaite, Stephen Bull, Simon Davies, Julian Saunders, Sylvia Hopkins, Jenny Spencer-Smith, Michael Ball, and Clare Wright. The Exhibition was brought to life by the Museum's designer John Quiddington, and the reconstructions were built by Paul Russell and Paul Tew. The conservation of exhibits was undertaken by Adrian Carlton, Susan Beale and Vincent Prior. This Publication was designed by Alastair Pether, assisted by Teresa Sullivan and written by David Smurthwaite, Mark Nicholls, and Linda Washington with expert contributions on their specialist subjects from Brigadier Kenneth Timbers, Colonel David Ronald, and

Lieutenant-Colonel George Forty. Photographs accompanying the Exhibition and Publication were prepared by Ian Jones.

In such a Special Exhibition, chronicling one of the greatest expeditionary armies ever sent by Britain to the Continent, advice has had to be sought from the Regimental and Corps Museums which record the history of the individual units. Many of them have organized their own events commemorating the start of the War but they have been generous in their replies and offer of items for display. We would like to thank all those who gave assistance and in particular the following individuals and Institutions:- Colonel P R Adair, The Guards Museum; Mr P Annis; Mr A Barratt; Miss C Buddin, Société Jersiaise; Colonel Sir Thomas Butler; Mr D Cohen; Mrs H R Cole, Guernsey Museum and Art Gallery; Brigadier A K Crawford and Major R W S Shaw, Intelligence Corps Museum; Mr M Dale, The Museum of the Royal Corps of Military Police; Mr C E Daniels; Colonel C D Darroch, The Royal Hampshire Regiment Museum; Brigadier E G Davies-Scourfield; Miss F Devereux, The Royal Fusiliers Regimental Museum; Lieutenant-Colonel G Forty, The Tank Museum, Bovington; Sir Martin Gilliat; Sir Basil Hall; Mr I Hook, The Essex Regiment Museum; The Imperial War Museum; Lieutenant-Colonel N D McIntosh, The Green Howards Museum; Mr J Mills; Lord Montagu of Beaulieu; Colonel P S Newton; Colonel D W Ronald and Mr W A Dugan, The Museum of Army Transport; Major R D W McLean, Museum of the Staffordshire Regiment; Brigadier K A Timbers and Mr S C Walter, The Royal Artillery Institution and Museum of Artillery; Major W H White, The Duke of Cornwall's Light Infantry Museum. The Colonel, 13/18th Royal Hussars kindly gave us permission to quote from the diaries of Trooper Munns. Our thanks also to Major - General R L Peck the Engineer-in-Chief for providing skilled Sapper assistance in constructing the Exhibition.

The reconstructions in the Special Exhibition were accompanied by examples of vehicles and weaponry of the period, a testament to a time when the Army was being mechanized and re-equipped on a massive scale. A particular expression of gratitude is due to the Directors and staff of Vanguard Engineering Ltd whose generous sponsorship enabled these vehicles, guns, and tanks to be transferred quickly and safely into the gallery.

Finally, it is hoped that this Publication in its New Edition, and the Special Exhibition it was produced to accompany, will be accepted as a tribute, however inadequate, to those who went off to fight in the British Army of 1939-40.

Ian G Robertson
Director, National Army Museum,
May 1990

3

'AGAINST ALL ODDS'

Attacks on the English homeland are to be prepared, bearing in mind that inconclusive results with insufficient forces are to be avoided in all circumstances

War Directive No 1 31 August 1939

The immediate aim of the German High Command remains the rapid and victorious conclusion of operations against Poland. The transfer of any considerable forces from the Eastern front to the West will not be made without my approval

War Directive No 2 3 September 1939

In our fight against the Western Powers England has shown herself to be the animator of the fighting spirit of the enemy and the leading enemy power. The defeat of England is essential to final victory

War Directive No 9 29 November 1939

4

The progress of the offensive to date shows that the enemy has failed to appreciate in time the basic idea of our operations. He continues to throw strong forces against the line Namur-Antwerp and appears to be neglecting the sector facing Army Group A

War Directive No 11 14 May 1940

The next object of our operations is to annihilate the French, English, and Belgian Forces which are surrounded in Artois and Flanders, by a concentric attack by our northern flank and by the swift seizure of the Channel coast in this area

War Directive No 13 24 May 1940

Since England, in spite of her hopeless military situation, shows no signs of being ready to come to an understanding, I have decided to prepare a landing operation against England, and, if necessary, to carry it out. The aim of this operation will be to eliminate the English homeland as a base for the prosecution of the war against Germany and, if necessary, to occupy it completely

War Directive No 16 16 July 1940

Source: Hugh Trevor-Roper (ed) *Hitler's War Directives 1939-45* London, Sidgwick and Jackson, 1964

'AGAINST ALL ODDS'

Territorial Army recruiting poster, No 6 of a series by Lance Cattermole (b.1898), published by the War Office in 1938 as part of an intensified recruitment campaign
National Army Museum 8401-54

'AGAINST ALL ODDS'

Britain's Post-1918 Army

In August 1914 the British Government despatched to Europe an Expeditionary Force of six infantry and one cavalry divisions composed entirely of professional troops. Over the next few years the 'Kitchener Armies', the dominions and colonies contributed hundreds of thousands of recruits to the forces, and by the end of the war Britain and her Empire deployed eighty infantry and eight cavalry divisions on active service outside the UK and India, of which sixty-one infantry and three cavalry divisions were serving on the Western Front. On the outbreak of war the total strength of the Regular Army, Reserves, and Territorial Forces had been 733,514, but four years later there were around 1,750,000 on the Western Front alone. Throughout the war a total of 5,500,000 troops had been deployed in France, at one point reaching a maximum of two million. This was reflected in the extent of the front-line held by British forces, which grew from 20-25 miles in 1914 to 123 miles in 1918. The price paid was correspondingly great and on all fronts over 700,000 men were killed, 150,000 posted as missing or prisoners, and 1,660,000 wounded.

The glory of victory rapidly faded and on the conclusion of peace there began a progressive decline in the size and quality of the Army. The practical need for financial caution was reinforced by revulsion against the mass slaughter on the Western Front, and optimism that a new era of international peace was now possible. In 1919 the Government issued the notorious 'Ten Year Rule' for defence spending which ordered that 'it should be assumed for framing revised estimates that the British Empire will not be engaged in any great war during the next ten years, and that no Expeditionary Force is required for this purpose'. For the next thirteen years competition with the other two services for limited funds ruined the Army's chances of expansion and modernization. Army estimates were reduced every year from 1923 to 1932, during which the Navy received an average annual allocation of £13 million for the purchase of armaments, the RAF £7 million, while the Army was allotted only £2 million. Practical evidence of this parsimony was soon forthcoming: in 1922 Sir Eric Geddes and the Committee on National Expenditure wielded the 'Geddes Axe' which resulted in the disbandment of twenty-two infantry battalions, the reduction of the cavalry from twenty-eight to twenty regiments and the withdrawal of seven battalions from overseas garrisons. Irish independence had forced the demise of the five Irish regiments but the others were clearly a case of economy taking precedence over military efficiency. The establishment of the Territorial Army was similarly reduced, dropping from 216,041 in 1922-3 to 184,161 in 1925-6.

After the Ten Year Rule was introduced revised priorities for home and overseas defence were established. Early in 1922 the Cabinet instructed the War Office that it should not provide for the contingency of another major European war but maintain home security and imperial defence, possibly providing an Expeditionary Force for a minor war outside Europe. Britain was retreating from any firm commitment to intervene in any European conflict and forcing the Army back to its nineteenth-century role as imperial policemen, though with insufficient resources for

> **66** *There is no actual rearmament in England, just propaganda ... The English speak a war of nerves* **99**
>
> *Adolf Hitler, speech to the Commanders-in-Chief, 22 Aug 1939*

commitments expanded by the occupation of the Rhineland and the acquisition of mandated territories in the Middle East.

Financial restrictions intensified a stagnation affecting the whole character and spirit of the Army. The malaise started at the top where the post of Secretary of State for War remained one of the least-desirable Cabinet posts, failing to attract first-rate ministers, while the War Office itself lived up to its reputation as unimaginative and indecisive. Promotion prospects were reduced by demobilization, and many able officers who hoped to make a career in the post-war Army found their path blocked by the surfeit of senior officers who moved sideways to different appointments until retirement, to be succeeded by only slightly-younger men. Archibald Wavell had been a brigadier-general in World War I but in 1920 rejoined his regiment as a major in command of a company, taking ten years to work his way back to his former rank. There developed a 'lost generation' of soldiers who did not reach senior rank until the late 1930s when they were past the peak of their capabilities. The ordinary recruit was deterred from joining up by low pay and a poor standard of living. From 1923 to 1932 the strength of the Army fell from 231,000 to 207,000.

With some notable exceptions, peacetime soldiering with its general lack of urgency was detrimental to the intellectual life of the Army and, though the last war was studied, few plans were made for the next. Adequate funding for technological research and development was not available and mechanization became the most obvious and serious victim of this financial blight. Though the Royal Tank Corps was established as a permanent branch of the Army, debates raged about the employment and tactics of mobile armoured units as the process of mechanization was delayed and Britain lost its place as the pioneer of armoured warfare. In 1933 there were 136 infantry battalions and eighteen horsed cavalry regiments but only four tank battalions and two regiments of armoured cars.

The End of the 'Ten Year Rule'

In 1933 Adolf Hitler became Chancellor of Germany and his country's rearmament process escalated in scale and speed. In December of that year he directed that the German Army, limited by the Treaty of Versailles, should be trebled and further expansions were followed by the reintroduction of conscription in 1935. By the summer of 1939 Germany had fifty-two active and fifty-one reserve divisions containing three-and-a-half million men, poised for use against Poland. By the time Hitler gained power the British inter-service Chiefs of Staff Committee (COS), worried by increasing international tension and particularly by Japan's menacing attitude, had successfully challenged the Ten Year Rule. In their annual review of 1932 they warned that if an Expeditionary Force were needed for Europe Britain could only contribute one division in the first month and three more to arrive piecemeal over the first four months. After reviewing the report the Government did not accept a commitment to send troops to the continent but instituted a deficiency programme which tried to fill the existing gaps in armaments and equipment.

While tension between Germany and France grew steadily the British Government evolved the policy of 'appeasement', trying to satisfy any German demands not directly disrupting the peace of Western Europe. The COS and the Defence Requirements Sub-Committee (DRC) continued to insist that in any European War Britain must be ready to protect the Low Countries, from which Germany would be able

8

Adolf Hitler, Führer of the Reich, and Benito Mussolini, Il Duce of Italy, attending German Army manoeuvres in 1937, two years before the Dictators signed the Pact of Steel
National Army Museum 8504-49-30

to launch an air attack on the United Kingdom. The third report of the DRC was examined between November 1935 and March 1936 against the background of German rearmament, Hitler's reoccupation of the previously-demilitarized Rhineland, and Italian aggression against Abyssinia. The report confirmed the priority of home and imperial defence but pressed the need to provide for a Field Force of one cavalry, four infantry divisions, and two air defence brigades, reinforced during the first eight months of war by twelve territorial divisions. The Government agreed to this 'continental commitment' in principle, but withheld the finance needed to equip the Force and the TA; the Navy and RAF continued to receive the largest percentage of the deficiency budget.

This 'limited liability' for a continental war was reduced to no liability in December 1937 when Prime Minister Neville Chamberlain and the Cabinet decided that the Army's most urgent tasks in war should be anti-aircraft defence and the reinforcement of imperial garrisons, followed by the despatch of the Field Force to an eastern theatre and, last of all, the continental commitment. The TA would remain at home to maintain order and essential services, and man anti-aircraft guns, rather than being equipped on a continental scale. In the following months weapons production gave priority to anti-aircraft guns, with serious consequences for the deficiency programme as a whole. As a result of the policy of limited liability none of the units allocated to the Field Force were equipped for war in Europe, nor was there provision for the trained reserves which would be needed to support the Field Force once hostilities began.

The 'Continental Commitment'

During the German annexation of Austria in March 1938 and the Munich conference over Czechoslovakia in September of that year the Chamberlain Government continued to appease Hitler and the crises had little effect on British strategy. However the German take-over in Czechoslovakia in March 1939 and the Italian invasion of Abyssinia forced a stiffening of attitude and public guarantees of aid to Poland, Greece, and Rumania if they were the victims of aggression. Over the next few months, after pressure from Paris, Anglo-French staff talks were held at a higher level and with wider scope than at any time in the last twenty years, starting with a discussion of overall strategy, then drawing broad outlines for individual theatres, and finally formulating detailed joint plans.

Allied discussions generally confirmed the strategy outlined by the British COS in their

9

From left: Brigadier Ridley Pakenham-Walsh, Eastern Command, General William Edmund Ironside, ADC General to the King, and Field Marshal Sir Cyril Deverell, the Chief of the Imperial General Staff, talking to Joachim von Ribbentrop, the German Ambassador to London, at German Army manoeuvres in 1937
National Army Museum 8504-49-28

A photograph taken at the Staff College showing officers who were to find fame or obscurity in World War II
(see note at end of chapter)
National Army Museum 6305-49

European Appreciation of February 1939 which remained valid to the outbreak of war. It took as the scenario an Anglo-French alliance against Germany and Italy, with the possible intervention of Japan, in a war caused by a German attack on France or the Low Countries in April 1939. German and Italian land forces would outnumber those of the Allies who would thus initially adopt a defensive strategy, securing home and overseas bases while checking the German offensive. As they strengthened the war economy and mobilized imperial forces for a land offensive the Navy and Air Force would wear down the enemy by blockading ports and bombing industrial areas. In the early stages the only possible land offensives would be against Italian garrisons in Libya and Abyssinia.

In the summer of 1939 British and French senior officers exchanged visits and views on how to contain the German offensive. Co-ordination would be achieved through a Supreme War Council of Anglo-French representatives and the Supreme Commander would be General Gamelin. The British Commander-in-Chief would be subordinate to General Georges, Commander of the Armies of the North-East, but would have the right of appeal to the British Government. The Allies' primary objective would be to maintain the integrity of French territory by basing a solid defence round the supposedly-impregnable Maginot Line, a system of fortifications stretching for 200 miles along the Franco-German frontier. If Belgium was invaded they would move forward to form a front on Belgian territory. The British Expeditionary Force would consist of four Regular divisions in the first six weeks of war, ten territorial divisions in four to six months, and the remaining sixteen divisions between the ninth and twelfth months.

As the continental commitment was finally endorsed by the politicians the Army faced a sudden transformation in its priorities, size, and strategic plans. On 22 February 1939 the Cabinet decided that the four infantry divisions of the Field Force and the armoured division should be provided with full equipment on a continental scale, and that war equipment and reserves would also be provided for four territorial divisions. In a startling public change of policy the Government announced on 29 March that the Territorial Army would be brought up to its war establishment and then doubled to 340,000 men. Chamberlain's resistance to conscription finally crumbled and the Military Training Act introduced in May compelled all males reaching the age of twenty to serve in the armed forces for six months with a further three and a half in the Reserve. On 15 July the first and only intake of 35,000 militiamen was called up for the Army and by the outbreak of war had completed basic training.

The Army which the conscripts joined was already undergoing a thorough transformation initiated in 1937 by the Secretary of State for War, Leslie Hore-Belisha, who wanted to make soldiering a more attractive profession for officers and other ranks. After a political purge of the Army Council he had replaced the 63-year-old Chief of the Imperial General Staff Sir Cyril Deverell with the 51-year-old General Viscount Gort, lowered the retiring age for senior ranks, reduced tenure of staff appointments, and abolished the half-pay system. Promotion was to be automatic after a certain number of years to ensure that every competent officer could reach the rank of major,

Men of the Territorial Army stationed at Beaulieu Abbey in 1938
Courtesy of Lord Montagu of Beaulieu

and a massive number of promotions was an immediate result. The soldier's pay was increased from two shillings (10 pence) a day in his first year to three shillings a day after three years, and a pension was introduced after twenty-one years service. The Army's public image was further improved by modern, centrally-heated barracks and better food. Once in the ranks the soldier encountered more-imaginative methods of basic training and fieldcraft, and an emphasis on a good standard of general education. Reforming zeal extended down to the introduction of a more attractive walking-out dress and the practical battledress.

In the summer of 1939 the Army tried to adjust to the rapid changes imposed on it for political reasons. The influx of new recruits had been introduced more in reaction to foreign and public pressure than professional advice and created near chaos with the huge demands for training, weapons, and equipment. In January 1939 the Regular Army had a strength of 227,000 men including British troops in India and Burma, and there was a TA of 204,000 men. The Army Reserve was 102,000 strong, the Supplementary Reserve 1,100, the Regular Army Reserve of Officers 9,400, the newly-formed female Auxiliary Territorial Service up to 17,600, and there was an Officer Emergency Reserve. On the eve of war the Regular Army totalled 258,000, including militiamen, and over 500,000 reservists and territorials had been mobilized.

Organization and re-equipment did not catch up with these rapid changes. The speed of mechanization had quickened in 1938 and on 4 April 1939 Hore-Belisha announced the formation of the Royal Armoured Corps which was to contain the RTC, redesignated as the Royal Tank Regiment, and the eighteen regiments of cavalry undergoing mechanization. By the outbreak of war only the Household Cavalry,

A significant factor in deterring potential recruits was the low standard of living in the Army. This extract from a recruiting brochure of 1939 shows the improved catering after the Hore-Belisha reforms
National Army Museum negative 62857

two Regular and eight Yeomanry regiments retained their horses. In 1938 it was decided to form Britain's first armoured division but this was not ready for the first eight months of war and the only tanks to cross the Channel with the BEF were one battalion of infantry support tanks and four Regular and three Yeomanry divisional cavalry regiments, equipped with light tanks. A second infantry support battalion arrived in May 1940. The picture of practical unpreparedness was reflected in the rate of weapons production for all branches. For example, in June 1939 there was a predicted requirement of 1,770 new 25-pounder guns but only 140 were expected by end of September.

This was the British Army which went to war on 3 September 1939, rapidly improvised until the last moment. General Sir Edmund Ironside was suddenly appointed as Chief of the Imperial General Staff, replacing General Gort who departed to command the Expeditionary Force. After a smooth passage the first contingents of the BEF landed at Cherbourg on 10 September and moved up to the assembly area at Le Mans. In subsequent months the Army was supplied with a constant stream of Regular and Territorial

reinforcements, provided for by a mass of parliamentary legislation. The National Registration Act established a register of all persons in the UK, and building on this the National Service Act required all males aged between eighteen and forty-one to serve in the armed forces. The Military and Air Forces Act extended all terms of service to cover the current emergency, while the Armed Forces (Conditions of Service) Act made any Territorial soldier liable for overseas posting. The existing regimental depots converted to training centres for new recruits and by January 1940 the main deficiencies in manpower establishments had been filled. After a twenty-year struggle in Whitehall politics the Army faced the ultimate threat to its survival.

Further Reading

Bond, B *British Military Policy Between the Two World Wars* Oxford, Clarendon Press, 1980

Carver, Field Marshal Lord *The Seven Ages of the British Army* London, Weidenfeld and Nicolson, 1984

Fraser, D *And We Shall Shock Them, The British Army in the Second World War* London, Hodder and Stoughton, 1983

Gibbs, N H *Grand Strategy, Vol 1* London, HMSO, 1976

Larsen, R H *The British Army and the theory of armoured warfare 1918-40* London, Associated University Presses, 1984

Perry, F W *The Commonwealth Armies, Manpower and Organisation in Two World Wars* Manchester University Press, 1988

Note: Officers with final rank, and appointment in 1939-40

Back row from left: unknown; Lieutenant General Sir C J S King (1890-1967) Colonel Royal Engineers 1937, Engineer-in-Chief 1941-44; General The Hon A G L McNaughton (1887-1966) Commanded 1st Division Canadian Overseas Force 1939-40, GOC VII Corps 1940; General Sir A F A N Thorne (1885-1970) Commanded 48th Division BEF 1939-40; Lieutenant-General A E Percival (1887-1966) Brigadier, General Staff I Corps 1939-40; Lieutenant-General L Carr (1886-1954) Assistant CIGS 1939-40, Commanded I Corps 1940-41; Lieutenant-General Sir O M Lund (1891-1956) Deputy Director of Operations War Office September 1939; Lieutenant-General C W M Norrie, 1st Baron Norrie, (1893-1977) Commanded 1st Armoured Brigade 1938-40; General Sir R L McCreery (1898-1967) GSOI 1st Division 1938-39, Commanded 2nd Armoured Brigade; General Sir J T Crocker (1896-1963) Commanded an Armoured Brigade in France, 1940; Lieutenant-General J L I Hawkesworth (1893-1945) Commanded 12th Brigade 1940, Director of Military Training 1940; Major-General M B Beckwith-Smith (1890-1942) Commanded 1st Guards Brigade, 1939-40.

Centre row: Lieutenant-General Sir G Le Q Martel (1889-1958) Deputy Director of Mechanization 1938-39, Commanded 50th (Northumbrian) Division 1939, Commanded Royal Armoured Corps 1940; Major-General V V Pope (1891-1941) Brigadier, General Staff Southern Command 1938; Lieutenant-General N M S Irwin (1892-1972) Commanded 6th Infantry Brigade 1939-40, 2nd Division 1940; Lieutenant-General M B Burrows (1894-1967) Military Attaché Rome, Budapest, and Tirana 1938-40; Major-General R J Collins (1880-1950) appointed GOC 61st Division September 1939, Commandant Staff College Camberley November 1939-41; Lieutenant-General H R S Massy (1884-1965) Deputy CIGS 1939-40; PC Maltby RAF; J L Storey RN; R H M S Saundby, RAF; Lieutenant-General H B D Willcox (1889-1968) Inspector of Infantry War Office 1939-40; Field Marshal Viscount Montgomery of Alamein (1887-1976) Commanded 3rd Division 1939-40, V Corps 1940.

Front row: General Sir B C T Paget (1887-1961) Commandant Staff College Camberley 1938-39 Commander 18th Division in Norway 1939-40; Field-Marshal Earl Alexander of Tunis (1891-1969) Commanded 1st Division 1938-40; Lieutenant-General Sir R F Adam (1885-1982) Commanded III Corps 1939-40; Brigadier General G C Williams (1860-1947); Field-Marshal The Viscount Gort (1886-1946) CIGS 1937-39, C-in-C BEF 1939-40; Field-Marshal Viscount Alanbrooke (1883-1963) GOC-in-C Southern Command 1939-40, Commanded II Corps 1939-40; General Sir R G Gordon-Finlayson (1881-1956) Adjutant-General to the Forces 1939-40; Lieutenant-General Sir R H Carrington (1882-1964) Deputy Adjutant-General 1939, GOC-in C Scottish Command 1940; Lieutenant-General Sir F P Nosworthy (1887-1971) Deputy Chief of General Staff India 1938-40; Lieutenant-General Sir W G Lindsell (1884-1973) Quartermaster General of the BEF.

13

The Aftermath of the Great War

5 November 1918 saw the last tank action of the Great War, when eight Whippets belonging to the 5th Battalion, Tank Corps, supported 3rd Guards Brigade near Mormal Forest, while the armoured cars of 17th Battalion, Tank Corps, operated in the vanguard of the final advance before the Armistice. Nearly 2,000 tanks and armoured cars had been fighting non-stop for ninety-six days, and, despite grievous casualties to men and vehicles, the Tank Corps had shown to everyone who cared to take notice that the armoured fighting vehicle had arrived and would have a major impact in future wars.

Unfortunately this fact was far more obvious to the beaten Germans than to the victorious British. On 2 October 1918, General Ludendorff, while reporting to the German Parliament, had said: 'there is no longer any prospect or possibility of compelling the enemy to make peace. Above all two facts have been decisive for this issue: first, the tanks...'. On the British side, however, the reaction was very different: 'Thank God we can now get back to some real soldiering!' said one officer to the military theorist and historian John Fuller, on the day the Armistice was signed. And that meant putting the horse back into its rightful place on the battlefield, while relegating those dirty, smelly machines as far away from 'real soldiers' as possible. This attitude of mind was assisted by the fact that tanks were costly to build and maintain, while the British Empire could be held together far more easily with inexpensive, easily-adaptable armoured cars and infantry.

> 66 *The best of all we had to give had gone to the British Expeditionary Force, and although they had not the numbers of tanks and some articles of equipment which were desirable, they were a very well and fully equipped Army* 99
>
> Churchill, 4 June 1940, House of Commons

At least we did not go as far as the Americans, who disbanded their infant Tank Corps, or the French who entirely subordinated theirs to the infantry. Nevertheless, the Tank Corps had to face considerable pressure from within the Army to get rid of it entirely. As it was, the Tank Corps was swiftly reduced from eighteen battalions to a mere four, and then had to live in constant danger of disbandment until it received the Royal seal of approval on 18 October 1923 and became the Royal Tank Corps (RTC). It was fortunate that George V had taken a keen interest in the Tank Corps ever since its inception and had more faith in the new arm than most of his generals!

Tank Design and Development

A tank has three basic characteristics, namely: firepower, protection, and mobility, the first of these being the most important. Indeed, a tank can best be described as a means of carrying protected firepower about on the battlefield, wherever and whenever it is needed. These three characteristics can be varied one against the other to produce, for example, light, medium, or heavy tanks, or mixed in an entirely different way to produce specialised armoured fighting vehicles, such as armoured cars, tank destroyers, or armoured personnel carriers.

Between the wars tank design was heavily influenced not only by the experience gained in the Great War, but also by factors such as shortage of finance, the need to police the Empire, and the inherent military prejudice of the period against all things mechanical.

Meanwhile, on the tactical side, tank pioneers such as Fuller, Basil Liddell-Hart, George Lindsay, Charles Broad, Giffard Martel, and later Percy Hobart, formulated basic tactics for tank formations and did all they could to promote the armoured fighting vehicle. Some of them were perhaps unduly influenced by the shortcomings of the Great War tanks, namely their slow speed, poor radius of action, and lack of manoeuvrability. To rectify these shortcomings it was decided that tanks had to become much smaller and no doubt this was warmly applauded by the Treasury, as smaller in those days definitely meant cheaper.

Without looking back too far, it will be useful at this juncture to remember some of the basic characteristics of the British heavy tank in service at the end of the Great War, to use as a yardstick by which to judge the inter-war development. The Heavy Mark V male tank weighed 29 tons, had armour between 6 and 12mm thick, a top speed of 4.6mph, a radius of action of only 45 miles, but was armed with two 6-pounder guns, capable of firing armour-piercing (AP), high explosive (HE) and cased shot, plus four machine guns. Bearing in mind that firepower is the *raison d'etre* of the tank, it is a sobering thought that not one single tank in British operational service ever approached a similar level of firepower until the arrival of the American M3 General Grant in the Western Desert in 1942.

Three Types of Tanks

It was considered that, for the varying roles which tanks were likely to have to perform on the battlefield, three very different types were

HM King George V, accompanied by Queen Mary, inspects a Vickers Medium Tank belonging to 2 RTC, Pinehurst Barracks, Aldershot, spring 1924
Courtesy of the Tank Museum

'AGAINST ALL ODDS'

needed, namely: light fast tanks for reconnaissance and similar missions; medium or cruiser tanks which were able to move swiftly about on the battlefield, yet had the necessary firepower and armoured protection to make their presence decisive in a tank battle; finally, the heavy or Infantry ('I') tank, which could provide close support for the infantry in both the assault and defence. It is sad to report that both designers and tacticians alike, aided and abetted by those who held the purse-strings, put firepower right at the bottom of their list of priorities. This did not matter in peacetime, but would put British armour at a serious disadvantage when the shooting war began.

Perhaps it would not have been so bad had armour been available in reasonable quantities, but this was not the case. While time and time again, the RTC's embryo armoured divisions defeated horse and foot soldiers alike, the results of such exercises were conveniently ignored by those in authority and there was no move to increase the size of the RTC or to speed up mechanization. It was perhaps doubly unfortunate that officers from the German Army witnessed these armoured successes and learned from them. Men like Heinz Guderian, 'Father of the *Panzerwaffe*', were not too proud to make use of the ideas of his erstwhile enemies, translating Broad's first mechanized warfare pamphlet 'Mechanised and Armoured Formations' and then issuing it to all his panzer forces as a basic training manual. While British tankmen were frustrated at every turn, the Germans were able to accept the new philosophy and to gain from it. They were of course fortunate to have Adolf Hitler as their patron, the *panzer* divisions quickly becoming his special favourites.

Likewise, German tank designers were unfettered by the constraints which were placed upon their British counterparts so were able, even in the early 1930's, to design and build tanks like the PzKpfw III and IV, which were capable of being constantly up-armoured and up-gunned, so that they remained in German service throughout most of the war. For example, the PzKpfw IV was first produced in 1935, yet it was still in quantity production in 1945. One of the main reasons for this was because it had been designed with a wide enough turret ring to be able to accept larger and larger main armaments. British tank designers seemed incapable of thinking big enough. Perhaps the only time they did so was when the 'Old Gang' who had designed the Great War heavy tanks, began designing TOG in 1939. At eighty tons it was the largest British tank ever built, but never went into production and was finally shelved in 1944. Sadly it was a dinosaur, a tank intended for World War II, yet based upon the theory and practice of World War I, so it was doomed from the very outset.

Light Tanks

The line of pre-war British light tanks sprang from the earlier little 'tankettes', designed and built by Martel and Carden-Lloyd in the 1920s, which also can be said to have been the ancestor of the carrier. Tankettes and then light tanks had the great advantage of being very cheap and easy to produce (Martel's tankette had cost under £500!). Weighing some four or five tons, the early light tanks were simple, basic vehicles, crewed by just two men, so the Commander had the utmost difficulty doing his job properly when he also had to fire the turret armament. They were built, like most other British tanks of the period, by Vickers Armstrong of Newcastle, who kept British tank building alive in the 1920s and 1930s.

Light tanks were the most numerous British

Light tanks of 6th Light Tank Company, RTC, on parade for the Commander-in-Chief, India, 28 February 1939
Courtesy of the Tank Museum

tanks between the wars so, despite their many disadvantages, they did enable the Tank Corps to train, and of course made it easier for the cavalry to mechanize when this became a necessity. Nevertheless, when the Secretary of State for War of 1936-7 had the gall to liken the mechanization of the cavalry to 'asking a great musical performer to throw away his violin and to devote himself in future to the gramophone', one can well imagine that the process was not an entirely happy one, lacking the support it needed from senior officers who should have known better. Despite all such efforts to prevent it happening, however, the cavalry was mechanized over the decade up to 1939, some regiments like the 11th Hussars and 12th Lancers making a superlative job of it, the former quickly becoming the best armoured car regiment in the world. The logical outcome was of course the formation of the Royal Armoured Corps on 4 April 1939, when the newly-mechanized regiments of cavalry were combined with the RTC battalions to form a single Corps.

The main model of light tank in service at the outbreak of war was the Light Mark VI, a three-man tank, mounting a .5 Vickers heavy machine gun (MK VIC had a 15mm Besa) and a .303 Vickers MG (7.92mm Besa on the Mk VIC), with armour from 4mm up to 14mm thick and weighing some five tons. It had a maximum speed of 25mph and a radius of action of 130 miles. Some 1,100 were in service in 1939 and half of these went to France with the BEF and later with the 1st Armoured Division, which was sent out to reinforce the BEF just before Dunkirk.

Cruiser Tanks

The main gun tank of the RTC in the 1920s and 1930s was the Vickers Medium Mk II, and, whilst proposed replacements such as the 16-ton Medium Mk III and the A1E1 'Independent' were abandoned due to financial cutbacks, the Mk IIs managed to stagger on right up to the outbreak of war, but never saw action. Their place in the armoured division was taken by the cruisers, the A9 being the first of these sorry vehicles to enter service in 1937. Weighing some 10 tons, its main armament was a 2-pounder QF gun (3.7in howitzer on the close support version) which, although it had a good anti-armour performance, was of far too small a calibre to fire an effective HE round. It had a crew of six, a top speed of 25mph, but armour no thicker than that of the light tank. Thus the A9 scored dangerously low marks on all counts, lacking in mobility, short on firepower and having little armoured protection - no wonder it was known as 'The Woolworth Tank'! 125

were built and some of the regiments in 1st Armoured Division had a proportion of A9s in France.

Next of the inadequate cruisers was the A10, basically an A9 with extra armour (now up to 30mm thick), which meant it was slower and less manoeuvrable than its predecessor. A10s were issued in 1939-40, in time for 1st Armoured Division to take some to France. Both the A9 and A10 had a complicated suspension, comprising triple-wheel bogies on springs, with Newton hydraulic shock absorbers, which gave them an indifferent cross-country performance. 175 were built.

The next cruiser to enter service had a radically-different suspension, featuring the Christie-type large roadwheels, which were to become so successful in the Russian BT series and then the battle-winning T34. The A13 had a top speed of 30mph, but its armour was still only 14mm thick. Powered by the Nuffield Liberty V12 340hp engine, the Cruiser Tank Mk III (A13) began a run of cruisers with the Christie-type suspension. Some A13s and the later up-armoured version, the A13 Mk II, were used in France in 1940, both being armed with the ubiquitous 2-pounder gun.

The Infantry Tank

It was in early 1934 that the Inspector-General of the RTC put forward a requirement for a tank designed specifically to co-operate with infantry. Two basic types were envisaged: the first was to be very heavily armoured, small and inconspicuous, armed only with machine guns and designed to deal with enemy infantry; the other would be larger, equally heavily armoured, but better-armed with heavier-calibre weapons, capable of dealing with enemy support

'Queen of the Battlefield', a Matilda Mk II goes through its paces, during training in 1940
Courtesy of the Tank Museum

weapons, including enemy tanks. Neither needed to be able to go very fast, as their speed of advance was geared entirely to that of the infantryman on his feet.

The two 'I' tanks produced were the A11 (Matilda I) and the A12 (Matilda II), the latter going on to earn the nickname 'Queen of the Desert' after its performance in North Africa against the Italians, where it reigned supreme until the dreaded German 88 Flak gun appeared on the scene in the anti-tank role. Matilda Mks I and II both saw service with the BEF in France, being the main equipment of the 4th and 7th Battalions RTR, which made up 1st Army Tank Brigade. Matilda I had a crew of only two, was armed with just one machine gun (either .5 or .303 Vickers), weighed eleven tons and had armour up to 60mm thick. Following the Dunkirk evacuation it went out of production, after a total of only 140 had been built.

Matilda II on the other hand, was un-doubtedly the best British tank of the 1939-40 era. Its thick armour (13mm up to 78mm) made it practically immune to German anti-tank guns, but like all British tanks of the period it lacked firepower, its main armament still being the 2-

pounder QF. Nearly 3,000 were built between 1938 and 1943, but only a handful were in service in 1940.

A third 'I' tank, the Vickers Valentine, was at that stage still on the drawing board, the first 'Infantry Tank Mk III' not being delivered to the Army until May 1940, so it played no part in the pre-Dunkirk period. It did, however, prove to be a satisfactory tank, remaining in production until 1944, by which time over 8,000 had been built.

Other Armoured Fighting Vehicles

Carriers As mentioned, the other line of development from the tankette was the carrier. There was little money available to enlarge these tiny AFVs in order to turn them into section-sized armoured personnel carriers, so instead they were used to move machine-gun teams about on the battlefield, for command and control, or for reconnaissance. As far as armoured formations were concerned, infantry travelled in soft-skinnned lorries for most of the war, as the carrier was unable to carry more than two or three men at a time. One version, the scout carrier, was used in fair numbers in the mechanized cavalry brigades of the BEF.

Armoured cars As explained, armoured cars were used to help police the Empire in the 1920s and 1930s, the RTC being allowed to expand with the formation of armoured car companies to man the elderly Austin, Rolls, and Crossley armoured cars in such far away places as India and China. When the cavalry mechanized, it was logical that some cavalry regiments should take over this role, while the RTC companies were re-equipped with light tanks. Nevertheless, Great Britain did not begin its wartime love affair with armoured cars until after the Blitzkrieg era, when they had seen how effective the large German eight-wheeled armoured cars could be even against tanks. The BEF took just one armoured car regiment to

A Vickers-Armstrong Mk IV Light Tank, one of the series developed from the Carden-Lloyd one-man tanks. Courtesy of the Tank Museum

France, while others were present in the Mobile Force in the Middle East.

In Action

The armoured units of the BEF *in toto*, consisted of 11 mechanized cavalry regiments and 5 battalions of the Royal Tank Regiment. The BEF order of battle contained the 1st and 2nd Light Armoured Reconnaissance Brigades (each of 2 divisional cavalry regiments, containing 28 light tanks, and 44 scout carriers), 1st Army Tank Brigade (2 tank battalions, each of 50 'I' tanks, 7 light tanks, and 8 scout carriers), 3 unbrigaded divisional cavalry regiments and one armoured car regiment (30 armoured cars). Arriving later was the 1st Armoured Division, containing 2nd Armoured Brigade (3 cavalry light tank regiments, each 58 light tanks, and 5 scout carriers, and 3rd Armoured Brigade (3 armoured regiments, each of 52 cruiser tanks and 10 scout cars).

In general terms British armour performed less than adequately in France. There were insufficient tanks available to make a major impact, except on one important occasion. The losses in crewmen were inevitably highest in the light tank units. However, it has to be said that the British light tanks were certainly no worse than their German equivalents, the PzKpfw 1 Ausf A and B, which suffered in the same way and were relegated to secondary roles from then on. The cruisers were on the whole disappointing, but it is difficult to see what they could have done, being just one dispersed armoured division against ten panzer divisions. French armour was on a par with German in both quantity and quality but lost out in command and control, tactical skill, and determination, being easily cut to ribbons on practically every occasion when they chose to stand and fight. There were times when French armour fought bravely and well, but on the whole they were so spread out in 'penny packets' as to provide no defence whatsoever against the hard driving, concentrated might of the Blitzkrieg's *Schwerpunkt*.

It must also be said that the senior British officers in the War Office and for that matter in the BEF, had not the slightest idea how they should use the little armour that was available to them. 1st Armoured Division, brought in at the last minute, never fought as a division but was instead frittered away piecemeal, on many occasions being used for purely-static defensive work (such as 3rd RTR's role at Calais and St Omer). The same sorry picture was repeated almost everywhere, some tanks even being destroyed by their crews, on orders from above, before they had fired a shot in anger.

The one highspot for British armour in France has to be the famous Arras counter-attack by 4th and 7th RTR, which had Rommel in a flat spin for a while, and so affected the German High Command as to make Hitler decide to issue his famous 'Halt' order. Some historians, Liddell-Hart included, think so highly of this operation as to credit the Matildas of the 4th and 7th with a feat which deserves a special place in tank history: 'It may well be asked', he wrote in his history of the RTR, 'whether two battalions have ever had such a tremendous effect on history as the 4th and 7th RTR achieved by their action at Arras. Their effect in saving the British Army from being cut off from its escape port provides ample justification for the view that if two well-equipped armoured divisions had been available the Battle of France might also have been saved.'

Armour Losses

It has been estimated that the BEF took a grand total of 704 tanks of all types to France.

The majority of these were of course light tanks and cruisers. Of these only six light and seven cruiser tanks, belonging to 1st Armoured Division, managed to escape. The rest were lost, many destroyed by their crews when they broke down - it has been calculated that some 75% had mechanical failures of one kind or another - the remainder being knocked out by enemy action. Very few remained fit enough to be pressed into German service.

An Unhappy Time

1939-40 was an unhappy time for British armour in Europe - how different from the Western Desert, where the legacy of Sir Percy Hobart would produce one of the finest armoured formations in the world, the 7th Armoured Division. Poor British tank design, pig-headed stubborness against mechanization and the general apathy of the 'Peace at any Price' syndrome, had left us well behind in the race, so that we started World War II at a grave disadvantage. The 'Back to 1914 Brigade' had much to answer for in those dark days of 1940 and we would have to depend to a great degree upon American-built tanks during the critical years that followed.

Further Reading

Crow, D *British and Commonwealth AFVs 1940-46* Windsor, Profile Publications, 1971

Crow, D *Tanks of World War II* Windsor, Profile Publications, 1979

Forty, George *The British Tank: A Photographic History* London, 1986

Forty, George *The Royal Tank Regiment, A Pictorial History 1916-1987* London, Guild Publishing, 1989

Fuller, J F C *On Future Warfare* London, Sifton Praed, 1928

Grove, Eric *World War II Tanks* London, Orbis, 1976

Liddell Hart, Basil *The Tanks* (2 Vols) London, Cassell, 1959

Macksey, K *A History of the Royal Armoured Corps, 1914-1975* Beaminster, Newtown Publications, 1983

Smither, A J *A New Excalibur: the development of the tank 1909-39* London, Leo Cooper, 1986

21

'AGAINST ALL ODDS'

Organization

When King George V conferred the title 'Royal' on the Army Service Corps in late-1918, the event coincided with a turning point in the development of Army logistics. Between 1914 and 1919 the Army's fleet of load-carrying vehicles had grown from a few hundreds of WD subsidy types impressed into government service at the outbreak of war to a fleet of over 100,000 internal-combustion vehicles of all types. The era of the horse-drawn gun and wagon was, for the British Army, drawing to a close.

Mechanization effectively had begun in 1903 with the formation of No 77 Mechanical Transport (MT) Company ASC which took over from the Royal Engineers the traction engines which the latter had operated at Chatham. By 1911 confidence in the internal-combustion engine had grown to the extent that large-scale use of motor vehicles in rear areas was seen to be practical.

Development of vehicles before 1914 was in the hands of the War Office Mechanical Transport Committee. Perhaps the greatest achievement of this committee was the successful implementation of a subsidy scheme, which by 1914 made available nearly 900 standardized vehicles. At the end of the war responsibility for trials and development reverted to the RASC MT School at Aldershot, from 1920 under the direction of the War Office MT Advisory Board - the successor to the pre-war MT Committee. The Advisory Board was chaired by the Director of Supplies and Transport and included both military members

66 *The probabilities are that in the future petrol-power will revolutionise the art of war as extensively as did the introduction of fire-arms* **99**

J F C Fuller On Future Warfare
London, 1928

and distinguished civilian engineers and academics. The RASC retained this responsibility for research and development until 1928 when the tasks were transferred to the Master General of the Ordnance's department as part of the general growth of mechanization now affecting other arms and services. The Advisory Board became part of the Mechanical Warfare Board (later known as 'The Mechanisation Board').

The RASC, immediately on its formation, implemented a programme of 'mechanization' with full responsibility for the selection, trial, issue, and maintenance of the Army's motor transport. During the 1920s, work at Aldershot was concentrated on improvements to vehicle mobility-tyres, suspension, transmissions were all tested. By the end of the decade specialized military off-road vehicles were emerging as a distinct group of designs. Components and complete vehicles were tested at Farnborough and on trials held in Wales and Scotland, in addition to testing overseas in Egypt and India.

The centre for most of this development work was the RASC Mechanical Transport School at Aldershot. Lieutenant-Colonel Niblett and the school staff first developed a pneumatic-tyred 3-ton truck, and then went on to perfect a twin-axle rear bogie with a torque reaction system to achieve better cross-country movement. But possibly more important in the long term was their work on pneumatic tyres for desert conditions. By the outbreak of World War II the 'balloon' tyre had been perfected and was quickly proven in battle during the North African campaigns.

The 8-cwt 4 x 2 Morris Commercial Truck
Courtesy of the Museum of Army Transport

Vehicles

The peacetime vehicle complement of the RASC was only about 2,000, stationed in garrisons worldwide. As a result vehicles were only purchased in small numbers - which were always insufficient for large-scale manoeuvres. Several firms, of which the Artillery Transport Company of York was perhaps best known, filled the gap by hiring vehicles to the Army for manoeuvres and Territorial Army training camps. Only with rearmament from 1938 did the number of vehicles start to increase significantly. By this time the War Office had standardized on 8-cwt, 15-cwt, 30-cwt, and 3-ton load capacity vehicles. Of these, the 8- and 15-cwt vehicles were generally assigned to field units as transport for wireless, support weapons, or unit stores. The larger sizes were used to move supplies and men into the forward areas and, in the case of the 3-ton capacity vehicle, could accept a range of specialist bodies (workshops, caravans, signals vehicles, and so on). The plan was to remove the cargo ('general service') bodies from selected trucks on mobilization and mount the specialist bodies. Thereafter some of these specialist vehicles remained in service for long periods - as late as the mid-1950s.

None of the standard vehicle range had front wheel drive - using the military convention they were '4 x 2' (four wheels of which two are driven) or in the 3-ton range - '6 x 4'. Off-road mobility was therefore limited. For command and liaison duties in front-line units motorcycles or motorcycle/sidecar combinations were the norm. Platoon or troop commanders were expected to learn to ride motorcycles, whilst at battalion level the colonel would be issued with a conventional civilian car - usually an Austin 8 horse power or Hillman 10hp.

The next common vehicle was the 'light utility' based on a similar series of 10hp and 12hp car chassis. Standard, Morris, Hillman, and Austin varieties were in common use. However, at the outbreak of war there were actually more impressed civilian vehicles in Army service than there were military designs. Indeed, the Army of 1939 went to war with a very high proportion of impressed and requisitioned vehicles because production resources in the UK could not meet the demands of the armed services.

By 1939 the Army had approximately 15,000 trucks of the 15-cwt capacity range. These had been developed during the 1930s and series

An 8-cwt 4 x 2 Morris Commercial used as a Radio Truck
Courtesy of the Museum of Army Transport

production began with the Morris 'Commercial' in 1934, followed by the Guy 'Ant' in 1936 and, perhaps best known of all, the Bedford MWD model - trialled in 1937 and 1938 though only small numbers were purchased before the outbreak of war. Of these pre-1939 vehicles, the great majority were lost or captured in France during the evacuation of Dunkirk in June 1940.

The story repeats itself with the larger (30-cwt and 3-ton) load-carrying vehicles. Heavy losses at Dunkirk led to much new production - mostly of the more versatile 3-ton range. But the 30-cwt had a long history; the Morris 'Commercial' designs were built throughout the 1930s to military orders and examples of early World War II models remained in military service until the mid-1960s.

Perhaps the most spectacular and certainly the largest of the Army's vehicles in 1939 were the tank transporters. At the outbreak of war two types had been developed to carry the tanks of the period. The 'Albion' 20-ton tractor and trailer (developed from a Heavy Artillery Tractor) was found to be inadequate and was later down-rated to 15 tons. Better known in

many ways and certainly longer lived was the Scammell 'Pioneer'. This began development in 1925-6 as a 6 x 4 truck for colonial and oilfield use, but was quickly adopted as a military tank transporter (examples were used by the RASC from 1928) and as a heavy artillery tractor.

Another whole family of vehicles were developed as gun tractors. In World War I many of the larger load-carrying trucks (especially the American FWD made by The Four Wheel Drive Auto Company of Wisconsin) were used as gun tractors, but the Royal Field Artillery still used horses generally and the heavy guns were moved by steam traction engines or tractors. An entirely new family of Field Artillery Tractors (FAT) was developed in the 1930s. The first into service in 1938 was the Guy 'Quad-Ant' - a robust all-wheel-drive tractor which could carry the gun crew and over 100 rounds of ammunition. This was soon followed by the equally well-known Morris 'Commercial' C8 Mk I FAT.

For heavy artillery the Scammell 'Pioneer' tractor (similar to the tank transporter tractor described above) was a well-established and widely-used design. Just coming into service in 1939 were the first examples of a new Medium Artillery Tractor which was to become a classic British military vehicle.

3-ton, six-wheeled Thornycroft 1927
Courtesy of the Museum of Army Transport

'AGAINST ALL ODDS'

This was the AEC 'Matador' - a simple but exceptionally-robust 4 x 4 truck fitted with a two-speed range gearbox, the AEC 0853 diesel engine, and a most-effective winch. It is this last feature which has led to the amazing survival of these World War II work-horses as timber haulers and as heavy breakdown vehicles. Technically it is interesting too, as the AEC design can be traced back through that firm's Slough plant to the Hardy Company. This firm bought surplus World War I FWD trucks from the huge stockpile of surplus equipment at the Slough depot, re-worked and sold them onto the civilian market after the Armistice.

Distribution

A word now about the provision of vehicles for Army use. The centre of RASC mechanical transport activity was the Vehicle Depot, Driver Training School and workshops at Feltham in Middlesex. To this depot were delivered all new WD vehicles and, following inspection and rectification of faults, Middlesex civilian registration numbers were applied. The WD 'Census' number was painted in small letters on the side of the vehicle body or cab.

Two styles were in general use - either an outlined oval with the census number in the centre and 'R.A.S.C.' and the unit designation round the perimeter or, for general use, a three-line designation with the abbreviated title of the user unit on the top line, the vehicle class letter below and then on the bottom line the vehicle census number. This style appears to have been in use by all arms except the RASC up till 1940. It is of interest that all Army vehicles carried appropriate signs and inscriptions for maximum speed, axle weights, etc, as laid down by the Road Traffic Acts. Divisional or formation signs were not painted on vehicles although their use - albeit unofficially - has been recorded during the Palestine Emergency of 1938.

This, then, was the mechanical transport fleet of the Army in 1939. 85,000 vehicles at the outbreak of the war is but nothing compared with over one-and-a-quarter million at the end of the war. The designs were generally well-proven, robust and simple, making best use of civilian components. Standard War Office bodies were used on a variety of makers' chassis. But the designs were generally outside the commercial range and British industry was not geared to meet the massive requirements from 1940 onwards. During the later years of the war many of the smaller groups of pre-1939 designs (eg 8-cwt load carriers) were phased out and genuine 'pre-war' designs were already relatively scarce by 1945.

The Morris 30-cwt 6 x 6 undergoing tests
Courtesy of the Museum of Army Transport

Further Reading

Crew, G *The Royal Army Service Corps* London, Leo Cooper, 1970

The Story of the Royal Army Service Corps 1939-1945 London, G Bell, 1955

Ellis, Chris *Military Transport of World War II* London, Blandford Press, 1971

25

The defeat of 1940 and the known inadequacies of aspects of the British Army have tended to overshadow that army's real achievements - achievements which would make their unmistakable appearance in the next few years.

Mobilization went smoothly, nowhere better than in the Artillery. Gunner units in the British Expeditionary Force were up to full war establishment and the same was true of the first Territorial units which joined them. Much of the Regiment's equipment was old but it had been well modernized in most cases. All units were mechanized - something which was not true of the artilleries of other countries - and the standard of training was excellent save for the aspects of communications and proper co-ordination with other arms. At the same time, however, attitudes both civil and military held during the period between the two world wars had some damaging effects.

Apart from relatively minor operations, where it had proved fully competent to play its part as an element of an imperial police force, the Regiment had experienced a time of peace in which it had not been idle. Building on the experience of the First World War and learning lessons from that conflict, the Regiment pursued a coherent and practical course. Institutions for education and training grew in number and the Royal Military Academy at Woolwich and the School of Artillery at Larkhill, in particular, earned enviable reputations. The concept of the provision of support for cavalry and infantry was well known and widely understood, it was after all the gunner's *raison d'etre*.

> 66 *Stories are gradually filtering through of the deeds of our artillerymen, fighting under difficult conditions, unforeseen circumstances and against heavy odds, deeds which stir and fill our hearts with pride and thankfulness* 99
>
> The Gunner *July 1940*

On the other hand, technical change, the growth of the tank arm, and the use of radio, had not been properly introduced into artillery doctrine. Funds had been short until about 1936 and there were too few trained soldiers and not enough thoroughly modern guns. In spite of great efforts by some forward-thinking officers the organization of the Regiment had also suffered and was not fully up to dealing with the sort of war which 1939 and 1940 demonstrated.

Artillery Regiments

A major organizational change was introduced in 1938. Prior to that artillery brigades, renamed artillery regiments in May 1938, were composed of four six-gun batteries. These were linked for the purpose of fire control by the brigade's own surveyors. The command radio link was provided by a team attached to each brigade from the Royal Corps of Signals. A battery's normal function was to support an infantry battalion, while the artillery brigade supported the infantry brigade composed of three such battalions. The Royal Horse Artillery provided a similar service for cavalry regiments and brigades. Medium and heavy artillery were directly under the command of the division or corps which incorporated the infantry and cavalry brigades.

The change of 1938 left the artillery regiment's number of guns, twenty-four, alone but now they were arranged into four six-gun troops, two of which formed a battery. Two batteries formed a regiment. The change was unpopular as flexibility and operational effectiveness were reduced. Three or more batteries could support

26

A 3-inch 20-cwt anti-aircraft gun (mobile), which was developed in World War I as the standard inter-service gun
Courtesy of the Royal Artillery Institution

three infantry battalions but two large batteries of the new type would have to be adjusted, in the possible presence of the enemy, to achieve the same result. The new batteries, being larger, had to be formed by combining existing ones, and as the battery had always been the focus of loyalty and thus an important element of morale, more damage was done. Yet there were some good features, the most important being that the new type of regiment could produce fire from more guns more quickly, and this approach was retained when the 1938 pattern of organization was dropped. The Regiment settled down to make the new system work and many gallant actions were fought under it in May 1940.

One of the reasons for the new scheme was that tactical doctrine was based largely on the concept of the advance. The brutal stalemate of the First World War was to be avoided and this was expected to be achieved by the aggressive use of armour, vehicle-borne infantry and highly-mobile and flexible artillery. None

of this was achieved; there simply was not enough of the material which might have made it work, nor were there sufficient men trained in the new doctrine. This state of affairs was redeemed to an extent by sound training and reliance on established principles which, if they were not that new, did work. Two examples stand out.

10th Field Regiment, RA, under the command of Lieutenant-Colonel H J Parham, was in a high state of efficiency. The commanding officer was a notable member of that group of artillery officers who had thought deeply about the future employment of the Regiment and its guns. In spite of all obstacles, 10th Field Regiment was also properly conversant with its radio communications. The regiment was deployed near the River Escaut but, thanks to the non-appearance of another unit, its flank was unprotected. One of Colonel Parham's observation officers suspected that enemy tanks were occupying a wood nearby and, thanks to proper communications, brought down 250

'AGAINST ALL ODDS'

rounds onto that wood. The results were spectacular as German tanks, ignorant of the British presence, were refuelling under cover of the trees. Colonel Parham observed that it made 'quite an impression on the spectators'. An historian, Brigadier Bidwell, pointed out that this was the 'first fully-predicted, radio-controlled concentration on an opportunity target ever fired by the Royal Artillery in war'. It augured well for the future.

A very different action took place on 27 May 1940 at Hondeghem where K Battery RHA, armed with the old 18-pounder Mark II and commanded by Major R R Hoare, was placed on one of the main German lines of advance. Major Hoare put the little village into a state of defence assisted by an officer and eighty men of an artillery searchlight unit, knowing that he could expect no other support. The Germans attacked early in the morning of 28 May. One troop of the battery was in and around the village and the other was sited on one flank. The German attack, in almost-overwhelming force, was held for eight hours with the 18-pounders firing as close as fifty yards from the British positions. The relative lightness of the British guns, as compared with their successors, enabled them to be manhandled from place to place and to be used where the attack was most threatening. Much of the fighting took place in the village and more German troops arrived. By mid-afternoon, with ammunition almost gone and many guns destroyed, the battery was ordered to fall back to the next village, St Sylvestre. That village was, however, occupied by German armour and infantry, and the battery began another action aided by a small party of men from the Royal Army Service Corps. One of K Battery's troop commanders, Captain N B C Teacher, led an assault on the German positions and charged through the village with his men mounted in the remaining vehicles. The survivors escaped in the gathering

A 2-pounder anti-tank gun in its firing position. The gun continued in production after the campaign in France
Courtesy of the Royal Artillery Institution

28

dark. These two actions demonstrate both the professionalism and the spirit of the Regiment in the gloom of defeat.

In 1939 the Regiment was divided into three discrete parts: field artillery (anti-tank, field, medium, and heavy), anti-aircraft artillery (light and heavy) and coast artillery. The last played no part in this story, but the other two were deeply involved and we should look at their equipments.

Guns in France

GUN	PROJECTILE	MAXIMUM RANGE (Yds)	REMARKS
2-pounder gun 1.57-inch	2.4 pounds armour-piercing	8,000 but 2,000 effective	Probably the best anti-tank gun in the world when introduced in 1938. The same size as German equivalents and soon outdated. The principal tank gun also.
18-pounder gun 3.3-inch	18.5 pounds, shrapnel or high explosive	9,300	The 1904 pattern field gun, modernized and fitted with pneumatic tyres.
18/25-pounder 3.45-inch	25 pounds high explosive	11,800	An interim design incorporating a 25-pounder gun on an 18-pounder carriage.
4.5-inch howitzer	35 pounds shrapnel or high explosive	7,000	The First World War field howitzer on pneumatic tyres.
60-pounder gun 5-inch	60 pounds	16,400	A First World War medium gun modernized and with pneumatic tyres.

6-inch 26-cwt howitzer	86 pounds	11,400	The other medium gun of the previous war, on pneumatic tyres.
8-inch howitzer Mark VIII	200 pounds	12,400	An obsolescent heavy howitzer on pneumatic tyres.
9.2-inch howitzer Mark II	290 pounds	13,900	Another heavy howitzer of the previous war now fitted with pneumatic tyres.
12-inch howitzer	750 pounds	14,350	Very difficult to move, the 'twelve-inch road hog', a 1917 design.

The guns listed are those which went to France, and some went only in very small numbers. Anti-aircraft artillery, designed for the protection of the Field Army, was represented by three types of gun. The figures for range represent the effective ceiling in feet.

40mm 1.57-inch	2 pounds	5,000	A Swedish design of 1928 on the open market in 1931. Made under licence in the UK but Swedish- and Polish-made examples also used. The basis of Light Anti-Aircraft (LAA) artillery. Also in use by the Germans.

3-inch 20-cwt	16 pounds	15,700	An Admiralty design of 1914, extensively modernized but becoming outmatched by later aircraft.
3.7-inch Mark III	28 pounds	32,000	An excellent original design which would get better and better.

The only truly modern guns to see service in France, therefore, were the 2-pounder anti-tank gun, the 40mm light anti-aircraft gun, and the 3.7-inch heavy anti-aircraft gun. German success in May 1940 led to the loss of nearly 2,000 guns, mostly of First World War origin but including 704 18/25-pounders and 509 2-pounder anti-tank guns, as well as the new anti-aircraft weapons. Many were destroyed in action and many others were left in a condition which rendered them of no use to their captors.

Transport

The other aspect of fairly-recent technological change involved the means whereby guns, ammunition, and supplies were moved to and on the battlefield. Until the middle 1930s the Regiment was largely dependent on horses for draught purposes. Medium and heavy guns had used a degree of mechanization since the war in South Africa and through the First World War, but field artillery was horse-drawn and guns and vehicles had large, spoked, wheels fitted with steel tyres. The decline in the number of horses available, as civil society mechanized, the knowledge that large numbers of horses placed heavy demands on logistic services and the slowness of horse-drawn vehicles meant that when money became available the Regiment was ready to accept mechanization and make it work. Although this did not begin until 1936, experiments, particularly in association with armour, had been conducted in the 1920s.

Within the Regiment was the vexed question of whether mechanical vehicles should be fitted with tracks or wheels. Many preferred tracks for their superior performance across country. At the same time, wheeled vehicles had improved remarkably with the fitting of pneumatic tyres and the provision of four-wheel drive. Furthermore, tracked vehicles had a reputation for unreliability. The elements of the Regiment which went to France were, therefore, mostly wheeled. Many vehicles were quite new and one of them, the Morris Four Wheel Drive Artillery Tractor, better known as the 'Quad', was to become pretty-well immortal, especially when associated with the Mark II 25-pounder. Mediums and some heavy guns were fortunate to have the Scammell tractor and other six-wheeled vehicles. One regiment in France had the 'Dragon' Mark III to tow its guns. This vehicle was based on the medium tank of the 1920s and, in some ways, had something to be said for it though it was very slow when towing a gun

25-pounder Mark I (also known as the 18/25-pounder) on 18-pounder carriage. The ammunition limber carries the traversing platform.
Courtesy of the Royal Artillery Institution

and its limber. Its unfortunate tendency towards spontaneous combustion meant that its users were hardly sorry when the few examples were abandoned in France.

The Regiment was equipped with radio which was reasonably effective if gently treated, and was a vital improvement on anything it had used before. Unhappily, for fear of German interception, the BEF were ordered to maintain radio silence during the period of the 'Phoney War', and consequent lack of experience in maintenance and use led to poor communications when the Germans attacked. The removal of regimental survey teams by the 1938 reorganization and sheer lack of experience in inter-arm co-operation all played their parts in the success enjoyed by the German Army.

The most important element of any army is its men. All regulars were superbly trained to unit level, their brethren in the first Territorial divisions to reach France were similarly of a very high standard, but there were too few of either. The Territorial Army was ordered to double in size in 1938 but little provision could be made to double the equipments and the training staff. The Regulars did all they could and this, allied to the enthusiasm and spirit of the Territorials led to remarkable results - but the German Army was ready for a major war and the British were not yet in that position.

In 1939 and 1940 the Regiment was not yet ready for the demands which would be placed on it. There were many reasons for this. The Regiment did its best in defeat and would later achieve greatness in victory, but this must have been unclear to those who had to destroy their guns and then wait on the beaches of north-western France at the end of May 1940.

Further Reading

Bidwell, Shelford and Graham, Dominick *Fire-Power, British Army Weapons and Theories of War 1904-1945* London, Allen and Unwin, 1982

Ellis, J *The Sharp End of War: the fighting man in World War II* Newton Abbott, David and Charles, 1980

History of the Royal Artillery 1919-39 Woolwich, Royal Artillery Institution, 1978

'AGAINST ALL ODDS'

Hogg, I V *Artillery in Colour, 1920-1963* Poole, Blandford Press, 1980

Hogg, I V *British and American Artillery of World War 2* London, Arms and Armour Press, 1978

James, N D G *Gunners at Larkhill* London, Gresham Books, 1983

Mead, P *Gunners at War 1939-1945* London, Ian Allan, 1982

Nicholson, C and Hughes, B P *The History of the Royal Artillery 1919-39* Woolwich, Royal Artillery Institution, 1978

Poston, M M; Hay, D; Scott, J D *Design and Development of Weapons: studies in government and industrial organization* London, HMSO, 1964

Terraine, J *White Heat: the new warfare 1914-18* London, Sidgwick and Jackson, 1982

Officers and men of 223 Battery 56th Anti-Tank Regiment, Royal Artillery, immediately prior to their embarkation for France to join the BEF in April 1940
National Army Museum Negative 72194

The infantryman has always been the human face of the British Army, dependable if unspectacular, employing simple but reliable weaponry, highly manoeuvrable in any terrain and presenting a small though vulnerable target. His public image, particularly before the First World War, has often been that of the least-skilled, and by inference the least-intelligent, individual in the Army. The Royal Artillery and Royal Engineers had always creamed off the best recruits for training at Woolwich, the Cavalry was a natural option for those with private means and superior education, and the Foot Guards also attracted men from the social élite. The Royal Artillery ended the First World War secure in its reputation and achievements and established a school of artillery to develop and teach new doctrines and technology, while the War Office and Cavalry spent the inter-war years engaged in a prolonged debate about the question of mechanization and the formation of armoured units. By comparison, the theory of infantry organization and tactics was the most neglected of any branch of the armed services and the birth of a school of infantry had to wait for the next war to pass. Though it was tacitly accepted that the basic formation of the Army would continue to be the infantry division with mechanized transport, not until the late 1930s did the War Office begin to prepare the foot-soldier for the challenges that lay ahead.

> **❝** *The Army is being mechanised. I hope it is being humanised* **❞**
>
> *Hore-Belisha, introducing Army Estimates, March 1939*

Organization

After World War I British Infantry was organized for 'small wars', the numerous campaigns which would have to be fought to defend and keep the peace all around the British Empire. Its size had been reduced by massive demobilization and the loss of twenty-two infantry battalions including the disbandment of five Irish regiments: the Royal Irish Regiment, the Connaught Rangers, the Prince of Wales's Leinster Regiment, the Royal Munster Fusiliers, and the Royal Dublin Fusiliers. The third and fourth battalions of the Royal Fusiliers, the Worcestershire Regiment, the Middlesex Regiment, the King's Royal Rifle Corps, and the Rifle Brigade were casualties of the economy drive being imposed on the War Office. A typical battalion headquarters contained nine officers and 129 other ranks, with four rifle companies, each of six officers, and 209 soldiers, many of whom were post-war new recruits. Until 1922 the heavy Vickers machine guns were concentrated in the Machine Gun Corps, whilst the infantry platoons contained two lighter Lewis machine gun sections and two rifle sections. The Corps was disbanded partly for financial reasons but also to release smaller units for employment all over Britain's scattered possessions by forming a machine gun platoon in every battalion, in 1928 these replaced a rifle company and seven years later were renamed battalion support companies.

By January 1939 the British Army contained five regiments of foot guards and sixty-four regiments of infantry, a total of 140 battalions, recently strengthened by the restoration or creation of second battalions to the Royal Inniskilling Fusiliers, the Royal Irish Fusiliers, the Irish and Welsh Guards. When it went to war in September the Expeditionary Force was organized as two Corps, each composed of three Regular infantry divisions, which in turn contained three infantry brigades of three battalions each, plus a brigade anti-tank company. Every division depended for heavy support on three Royal Artillery regiments and

Territorial Army recruiting poster No 7 by Lance Cattermole, published in 1938, showing infantrymen in service dress training with the standard Lee Enfield rifle and the new Bren Gun
National Army Museum 8805-29

'AGAINST ALL ODDS'

three Royal Engineer companies. However, reforms instituted by the War Office in the late 1930s had attempted to make the infantry more mobile and self-supporting in action. Some of the changes were the result of a new establishment coinciding with widespread mechanization and the issue of new armaments which affected all units, but a number of regiments were converted to more specialized roles. By 1939 there were three types of infantry unit: fifty-eight rifle regiments, four machine gun regiments and two motor regiments.

The new establishment of the standard infantry battalion was approved in 1937 and expanded slightly over the next two years, though no substantial alterations were necessary until 1943. When the War began a Battalion Headquarters was composed of four officers and forty-two other ranks, supported by a Headquarters Company running six platoons: Signals, Mortars, Anti-Aircraft, Pioneer, Carriers, plus the Administrative Platoon to which was attached the chaplain and men dealing with transport, stores, cooking, and medical services. The Signals and Carriers Platoons were commanded by officers, the Anti-Aircraft, Mortars, and Pioneer Platoons were led by platoon sergeant-majors, a rank recently introduced to compensate for the lack of young officers, and the number of other ranks in the platoons ranged between fourteen and thirty-three. Each of the four rifle companies had a headquarters of two captains, a company sergeant-major, a quartermaster-sergeant, and six soldiers. Manpower shortages sometimes reduced the four platoons to three, one of thirty men commanded by an officer, the other two with twenty-nine men led by a platoon sergeant-major, equipped with an anti-tank rifle, light machine guns and rifles. The transport for each battalion numbered over eighty vehicles, including fourteen motorcycles, and a combination of 8-cwt, 15-cwt and 30-cwt trucks and an office vehicle. The Carriers Platoon controlled ten carriers used for reconnaissance duties, each armed with a light machine-gun. Food supplies were carried in two Royal Army Service Corps 3-ton trucks and two water carts.

The standard Rifle Regiments found their capabilities expanded by the newly-arrived vehicles and weaponry which made the battalion a much more manouevrable body, controlling its own miniature artillery and armour. The BEF battalions had a total strength of approximately 780 men armed with 734 rifles, 50 light machine guns, two 3-inch mortars, 12 2-inch mortars and 22 anti-tank rifles. The 1st Bn The Duke of Wellington's Regiment had served the peacetime years at home and in Malta, but was back at Bordon in the United Kingdom when mechanization and new equipment arrived. On 24 September 1939 it embarked for Cherbourg, as part of the 3rd Brigade of the 1st Division of I Corps along with the 2nd Bn The Sherwood Foresters and 1st Bn The King's Shropshire Light Infantry. At Cobrieux near the Belgian frontier the battalion proceeded to dig its portion of the defensive 'Gort Line' until the end of November when the 3rd Infantry Brigade became the first British force to take a turn guarding a portion of the ultimately-futile Maginot Line. The historian of the regiment commented that it was a period 'chiefly remarkable for the extreme cold, and general discomfort of the forward troops' and the only offensive work they undertook was a listening patrol into enemy territory.

The War Office had originally intended to convert over a dozen regiments to a machine-gun role but this would have left too few rifle battalions for a Field Force destined for Europe, which by 1937 was becoming an increasingly likely prospect. Eventually only four infantry

Men of the 3rd County of London Yeomanry wearing the new battledress issued to all branches of the Army in 1939, as a more practical uniform for active service with new weapons and equipment
National Army Museum 7503-63-1

'AGAINST ALL ODDS'

regiments were selected to make the transition: the Royal Northumberland Fusiliers, the Middlesex Regiment, the Cheshire Regiment and the Manchester Regiment completed the changeover by 1938 and all continued in the machine gun role throughout the War. In the BEF three machine gun battalions were attached at Corps level to give the maximum degree of flexibility in the order of battle. Each of them had forty-eight medium machine guns and as additional weapons, 175 pistols, 559 rifles and 18 light machine guns.

One of the first machine gun battalions to sail with the BEF was the 2nd Bn The Royal Northumberland Fusiliers. The 1st Bn had been in Egypt in 1936 when officers and NCOs were sent to the United Kingdom for machine gun courses, and during the next year the horse-drawn transport was replaced by mechanized vehicles. It received the new equipment in abundance but the 2nd Battalion, which was at Bordon, found its conversion handicapped by a general lack of weapons and transport. Both battalions temporarily reverted to their standard infantry role for anti-terrorist operations in Palestine, but in the summer of 1939 reservists were being called up for training with the unfamiliar machines and vehicles. On 27 September 1939 the vehicle party of the 2nd Bn embarked for France, soon followed by their comrades, and the unit moved up to Tourcoing where it remained until 10 May 1940, spending the bulk of the time helping to construct defences along the Franco-Belgian frontier, with two weeks at Dannes for field firing and one week on field training near St Pol. From December one company at a time visited the Saar area of the French front and occupied positions on the Maginot Line. During the advance into Belgium the 2nd and 4th Bns (which had arrived in January 1940) were given the tasks of protecting and regulating the routes by which the BEF was to move, guarding vulnerable points, anti-parachute duties and control of traffic and refugees.

Armoured formations were closely supported by the third type of infantry unit, the Motor Regiment, which was intended to be fully mobile to keep up with the advance. A Motor Battalion consisted of the Headquarters and Headquarters Company, and three or four Motor Companies, each with three Mortar Platoons and one Scout Platoon and a Support Company containing the mortar, medium machine gun and anti-tank platoons, and equipped with 15-cwt trucks, carriers, jeeps and scout cars. These infantrymen could move and communicate quickly, being expected to be proficient with the wireless and handling signals. Their main role was to carry out patrols, to overcome obstacles to the armoured advance, to clear woods and built-up areas, hold rivers, capture positions and take care of prisoners. Down to platoon and even section level, units would be as independent and self-supporting as possible, carrying their own ammunition, food, water and cooking equipment.

These Motor Regiments were formed from the King's Royal Rifle Corps (KRRC) and the Rifle Brigade, the transition to the new form being accompanied by intensive training in driving and maintenance of vehicles, and in signals. In 1938 the 2nd KRRC had eighty vehicles but had not received the new light machine guns and had only a few anti-tank rifles. The battalion formed part of the 1st Armoured Division which did not accompany the BEF to France but continued training whilst waiting to be fully equipped. In April 1940 the KRRC was joined by the 1st Bn The Rifle Brigade and 1st Queen Victoria's Rifles, a territorial battalion of the KRRC, to form 30th Brigade. A month later, as the

The Boys .55 inch anti-tank rifle, the standard infantry anti-tank weapon carried by the British Army in the campaigns of 1940
National Army Museum 6405-60-69

Germans pushed towards the coast, the brigade and a light tank regiment were despatched to Calais in a vain attempt to help the BEF to break out - an attempt which resulted in the death or capture of the majority of the officers and men.

Some of the battalions with the BEF were organized as motorcycle battalions, about 550 strong, equipped for rapid, agile movement with 11 scout cars, 99 motorcycle/sidecar combinations and 43 motorcycles, and armed for maximum mobility with over 200 pistols and 300 rifles as personal weapons, plus 43 light machine guns, nine 2-inch mortars and 17 anti-tank rifles. The 4th Royal Northumberland Fusiliers, a territorial unit embodied on 1 September 1939, went to France in January 1940 as a motorcycle reconnaissance battalion of the 50th Division. During the move forward into Belgium it was used to maintain contact between static posts, protect bridges and vulnerable points, while the scout car platoons protected the routes against airborne attack, and provided refugee control.

Weapons

A closer look at the range of armaments available to the British infantryman in 1939-40 reveals that his transition from trench warfare to mobile tactics was still in its early stages. The rifle remained the foundation of the infantryman's equipment and training which every soldier was expected to be able to use efficiently if the need arose. In the inter-war years the War Office had investigated a variety of automatic or self-loading rifles but none had satisfied fears about reliability, so World War II was fought entirely with the bolt-action Lee Enfield rifle, which had first been introduced into the army in 1895 and technically had advanced very little since 1918. The BEF used the Mk III version, weighing around 9lb, and including a projecting muzzle onto which a 17-inch bayonet could be fixed, though this was rarely used. The Lee Enfield performed so well that soldiers rarely looted rifles from allies or enemies. The German Army made more use of the pistol than did the British infantry, where its use was often restricted to officers and specialists who could not carry rifles, and to armoured formations which found it more convenient to carry in tanks. It required more training and skill than a rifle and was a difficult weapon to fire accurately. By 1939 the powerful World War 1 .455 calibre pistol had been replaced by the .38 Enfield which remained

'AGAINST ALL ODDS'

standard issue throughout the war.

The machine guns of the early twentieth century, the water-cooled Maxim, Vickers and Browning, were used almost as artillery, carefully positioned to deliver long-range sustained fire to break up enemy formations and mow down advancing infantry. The Vickers Mark I .303 machine gun, dating from 1912, continued to be used by British infantry regiments throughout the war. Weighing 40lb and firing 450rpm it was extremely reliable in action, even in long periods of continuous fire. But in 1939-40 the British infantryman was also armed with the latest development in light machine guns, the Bren Gun, which replaced the obsolete Lewis Gun, and at 22lb was considered lightweight and mobile enough to be carried forward in battle, particularly when mounted in its own small armoured carrier. It was the finest of its type then available to any of the combatant nations, a gas-operated .303 calibre weapon firing 500 rounds per minute, sturdy, accurate, and reliable. The battle in France revealed the unsuitability of the medium machine gun and the future lay with the Bren and the new sub-machine gun, the Sten, which was adopted in 1941.

After rejecting the proposed adoption of the 2-pounder anti-tank gun, the infantry had no effective defence against tanks in the early part of the war. If an enemy tank evaded Royal Artillery and armoured formations the infantry employed the Boys Anti-Tank Rifle, approved for service in 1937, which could pierce 15mm tank armour at 250 yards with a steel-cored bullet fired at 325 feet per second, causing a tremendous recoil against the user. At 36lb in weight it was difficult to manoeuvre and was best directed from an entrenched position against the oncoming enemy, so it proved ineffective against blitzkrieg attacks and thickening tank armour.

Mortars were the infantry's artillery, a smooth-bore tube on a baseplate and supported by a bipod, which fired projectiles at angles of elevation between 45 and 90 degrees. The 3-inch mortar had a range of 1,600 yards, later extended to 2,800 yards, but it weighed 112 pounds in action and a lighter 2-inch mortar was put into production in 1938. With a small baseplate this weighed only ten-and-a-half pounds and by the outbreak of war was part of the standard equipment of every infantry platoon, capable of firing two and a quarter pounds of high explosive over a range of 500 yards.

The grenade was the lightest weapon available to the infantryman and, apart from the rarely-used bayonet, the one which had to be employed at close range. The standard British grenade was the 36M grenade, known as the 'Mills Bomb', which was used in every theatre of war. Weighing one pound 11oz with a four or seven second delay, the user had to ensure that there was adequate cover for himself as it was serrated for maximum fragmentation against the target, with some pieces thrown up to a hundred yards.

Traditionally the infantryman is thought of as the foot-slogging soldier equipped with the rifle and pack, though by the end of the Second World War he had to master an array of weapons, vehicles and tactics as varied and complex as that of any other branch of the army. In 1939-40 some of his weapons were not much more sophisticated than those employed on the Somme, but this period marked the transition from heavier armaments to those which could keep up with mechanized, armoured tactics, a process hastened by the experiences in France and the loss of so much valuable equipment during the evacuation from Dunkirk.

Further Reading

Barclay, C N *The History of the Duke of Wellington's Regiment 1919-1952* London, William Clowes, 1953

Barclay, C N *The History of the Royal Northumberland Fusiliers* London, William Clowes, 1952

Bidwell, S and Graham D, *Fire-Power, British Army Weapons and Theories of War 1904-1945* London, Allen and Unwin, 1982

Bryant, Arthur *Jackets of Green, A Study of the History, Philosophy and Character of the Rifle Brigade* London, Collins, 1972

Ellis, L F *The War in France and Flanders* London, HMSO, 1953

Hastings, Major R H W S *The Rifle Brigade in the Second World War* Aldershot, Gale and Polden, 1950

Hogg, I V *The Encyclopedia of Infantry Weapons of World War II* London, Arms and Armour Press, 1977

Myatt, Frederick *The British Infantry, 1660-1945* Poole, Blandford Press, 1983

Wake, Major-General H *Swift and Bold, The Story of the King's Royal Rifle Corps in the Second World War 1939-1945* Aldershot, Gale and Polden, 1949

41

13th Frontier Force Rifles training with the Vickers Gun, *circa* 1938
National Army Museum 6504-64-41

'AGAINST ALL ODDS'

The wide range of supporting Corps and services of the Army suffered perhaps more seriously from the inter-war lack of finance than the infantry, as their development depended more heavily on the purchase of modern technical equipment and on being able to attract skilled professional recruits. However the deficiency programmes of the mid-1930s and the gradual increase of resources enabled most of the Corps to remedy their immediate problems and carry out their commitments in September 1939. The Allies failed to stop the German Army in 1940 because they planned for the wrong kind of war, misdirecting the resources into a static defensive line while Germany poured vaster quantities into a rapid, mobile 'lightning war'. A brief survey of the main Corps with units in France reveals no instances of the Corps being unable to meet their obligations under Allied plans to an extent which materially affected the course of the campaign.

> **66** *This is a fortress war. The House can see in its mind's eye the busy work of our soldiers, digging and building. Under their hands blockhouses and pill-boxes take shape, and with digging machines and with squelching spades they throw up breastworks or carve out entrenchments* **99**
>
> *Hore-Belisha, House of Commons, 22 November 1939*

created a heavy drain on trained men who were needed for supervision and instruction. In Britain the priority was to build new camps for recruits, improve barracks, and to strengthen home defences. Early in the war a programme to provide thirty-five training camps for infantry to accommodate 110,000 men was launched, to be followed by another of almost equal extent in the spring of 1940. New and extended administrative depots, were constructed, including big ordnance stores at Chilwell and Barry. In terms of domestic defence the emphasis was on the increase of anti-aircraft sites with associated facilities. The departure of the British Expeditionary Force to France left an inadequate number of RE personnel to carry on this programme and men with civil experience of construction work were recruited as officers, though it took time to train them in military methods.

Engineers at War

Of all the Corps and supporting services which operated in the United Kingdom and France the most essential for operational purposes was the Corps of Royal Engineers, which has the appropriate motto *Ubique* or 'Everywhere'. It accompanied the fighting arms to every theatre of war where it provided accommodation and facilities for troops and extended the roads and railways necessary for their deployment. The doubling of the Territorial Army and the introduction of compulsory service increased the available manpower but

Royal Engineer units accompanied the fighting arms to Norway for a rapidly-moving campaign during which no large-scale engineering contribution was demanded. By contrast, in France the BEF took over a sector of the line, for most of its length running along the Belgian frontier, where the Royal Engineers began to strengthen the existing fortifications which consisted of a partially-completed anti-tank ditch flanked about every 800 yards by a medium-sized concrete pillbox equipped with anti-tank weapons and occasionally with machine guns. 'X' Force, composed of Territorial units, decided to build a series of smaller concrete pillboxes in depth throughout the line and by the time the German

42

The Army's pressing need to attract skilled manpower during the inter-war years is vividly reflected in this RAOC recruiting poster of 1927
National Army Museum 8311-141

'AGAINST ALL ODDS'

A Despatch Rider of the Royal Signals during the evacuation from Dunkirk, 1940. Oil on canvas by Alfred Reginald Thomson (b.1894)
National Army Museum 8506-1

'AGAINST ALL ODDS'

offensive started over 400 pillboxes had been completed with another 100 in various stages of construction.

The pillboxes were reinforced with a network of anti-tank obstacles, utilising existing streams and rivers, as well as 40 miles of newly excavated and revetted ditches. Many were dug manually but the scale of the work prompted the creation of a new excavator company for which operators were drawn from all arms of the BEF and trained on the spot. Anti-tank road blocks were constructed and minefield sites selected, though no mines were laid because of the danger to civilian life which went on as normal in the surrounding countryside.

In November 1939 the RAF requested the provision of twenty-five aerodromes and twenty-five satellite fields in the next twelve months. The Royal Engineers were to provide the labour and material for these, resulting in a manpower crisis which prompted the formation of sixty new companies, with men recruited from the building trades and local councils. Very few had military experience before they were shipped out to France, but the emergency measures worked and by May twenty-one main fields and eight satellites were ready, and seven more could be made operable within two weeks.

The size of the BEF put considerable strain on housing and transport in France, detracting from vital defence work. On the expectation that the French could provide sufficient accommodation the British Army reserve of hutting had been allowed to dwindle and the engineers had to convert existing buildings in towns. Secure underground dugouts were provided for some of the principal headquarters by tunnelling companies; the GHQ at Doullens

extended to seventy chambers. It had already been agreed with the French that the British Army would construct any additional railway facilities required, and a 141 miles of track were laid.

As the Germans by-passed the Allied defences and penetrated deep into France, the engineers tried to slow the advance by constructing anti-tank obstacles on the defensive positions and demolishing bridges. At least 620 bridges were successfully blown during the three weeks before the evacuation from Dunkirk. Often there was a race with the enemy to seize the bridges: at one bridge near Blaringen RE units fought off German troops and then drove a lorry loaded with explosives onto the centre span where it was detonated. At Dunkirk, RE ingenuity helped the evacuation as men were ferried out to the larger ships by sappers in folding boats, and a jetty was constructed from 3-ton lorries driven into the sea at low tide with planks over the canopy frames. During the final phase of the campaign

A Military Policeman on medical duty, with a dog used to carry medical supplies, 1926
National Army Museum 7711-118-5

'AGAINST ALL ODDS'

the Corps undertook offensive operations to deprive the enemy of some of the spoils of war. Kent Fortress RE units sailed from the UK and destroyed large storage installations of oil and petrol in Amsterdam, Rotterdam, Antwerp, and on the Seine between Le Havre and Paris.

Communications, Transport and Supplies

While the engineers maintained the physical links between army units a more direct method of communication was supplied by the Royal Corps of Signals, formed in 1920. The size and science of wireless communications networks developed so rapidly that in World War II the Corps was to expand from a permanent establishment of 541 officers and 9,837 soldiers to 8,518 officers and 142,472 soldiers. However at the start of the War the financial limitations of the inter-war years meant that the general organization and equipment could not keep pace with the massive demands made of it. In the original BEF there were ten signal regiments, only four of which were Regular units. In the long static phase of the campaign the signals staff were able to train but became unduly dependent on lined communications and were not prepared to make the best use of wireless during the mobile phase, throwing a heavier load on signal despatch riders. The restricted number of sets covered the main command links but left nothing for administrative and liaison purposes, and lacked sufficient range.

Weapons and other warlike stores on which the troops depended for survival were supplied and maintained in working order by the Royal Army Ordnance Corps, which set up a Base Ordnance Depot and Base Ordnance Workshop at Nantes and a series of smaller bases behind the front line. Repairs were carried out by the 7,000 artificers and armourers of the RAOC(E) who were attached to each major fighting unit.

Their numbers were too few for effective workshop and recovery support, particularly in the bad winter which set in that year, and by February 1940 half of the unit transport of the BEF was off the road awaiting repair.

The Royal Army Service Corps which transported and supplied troops went to war as a fully-mechanized unit. In Norway it suffered particular limitations because of the difficult terrain and poor road conditions caused by frost and snow. In France each of the two corps and four divisions were to be provided with a RASC headquarters and three transport companies, one for ammunition, one for petrol, spare blankets and anti-gas stores, and the third for food. Each corps was also allotted two 'park' companies for holding reserves of ammunition and petrol. Five companies were used for the carriage of casualties, while four were reserved for troop-carrying and one for bridging material, and there were seven companies for general duties on the lines of communication. Eventually, over fifty companies were required to support the BEF. The Corps proved its effectiveness in the early days of the war, when by the end of October a supply of thirty days food for 250,000 men had been safely landed and stored. Other essential supplies to sustain morale were delivered by the Royal Army Pay Corps, the 'Quill Drivers', which sent a Command Pay Office, a Base Clearing House, a base cash office and seven field cash offices.

Mechanization of armoured fighting vehicles and transport had by 1939 reduced the need for the services of the Royal Army Veterinary Corps, a rare example of dwindling finance reflecting declining requirements. In September 1939 the complement of forty-two officers and 441 other ranks, was sufficient for immediate needs, including veterinary service for the 1st

Men of the North Staffordshire Regiment undergo the rigours of physical training, 1935
National Army Museum negative 4740

Cavalry Division which was sent to Palestine and whose formation raised the Army's horse strength from 2,600 to 11,600. However it was recognized that mechanical transport was not infallible and in October 1939 the Army decided that the BEF would need 500 pack animals for each front-line division to carry ammunition and supplies to positions inaccessible to wheeled traffic. India provided four animal-transport companies and a remount unit and mules for two Cypriot pack-transport units - a total of 2,700 animals, with accompanying vets.

The flow of this vast amount of men, equipment and supplies was directed by the Corps of Military Police, in addition to their task of maintaining discipline among the troops, and other policing duties. From a strength of 3,000 it provided field formation companies for the corps, divisions, and lines of communication. Additional labour for all types of Army projects in the UK and France was provided by the Auxiliary Military Pioneer Corps, which was formed in October 1939 and by the end of the year supplied 18,600 men in France, moving stores and carrying out manual jobs to

relieve fighting troops. More skilled tasks were performed by the women of the Auxiliary Territorial Service formed in September 1938. In the United Kingdom they were to serve in a variety of roles, including as anti-aircraft crew, but had only a short stay in France, as bilingual telephonists in Paris, Dieppe, and Nantes.

The Soldier's Welfare

When housed, equipped, fed, and paid, the further physical care of the troops was provided by the Royal Army Medical Corps, also a victim of the savage cut-backs of the inter-war years. This highly-skilled corps suffered a lack of recruits because it offered insufficient professional opportunity, economic attraction and status, when compared to civilian life. Nevertheless the RAMC rose to the challenge, providing the BEF with nearly 1,000 officers and 8,000 other ranks to staff GHQ and other formations, and raised 64 field medical units. An advance party of senior RAMC officers reached the assembly area at Le Mans on 4 September, the day after war was declared. During the German offensive of May 1940 the medical teams succeeded in evacuating the majority of casualties through confused or disrupted lines of communication; at Dunkirk stretchers were loaded onto boats from an open beach, often under fire. The dedication and gallantry with which they cared for the casualties was vividly demonstrated on 1 June when 12 Casualty Clearing Station drew lots to decide which three officers and thirty men should be left to go into captivity with the wounded. The men selected uncomplainingly accepted their fate.

The Army Dental Corps supplemented the work of the RAMC in keeping the men fighting fit. For a field force serving overseas a ratio of one dental officer to 1,500 men was recommended, but the Corps was unable to achieve the desired proportions and by October there were only thirty-two grossly-overworked officers for 158,000 men, a ratio which resulted in considerable discomfort for many sufferers. Similar dedication to the personal welfare of the troops was provided by the Royal Army Chaplains' Department which encompassed all the main denominations of the United Kingdom. In 1939 there were 169 Protestant chaplains, 20 Roman Catholic priests, plus about 100 TA chaplains and a few in the Reserve forces. Like the medical units these men shared the fate of the men to whom they had been assigned and by the end of the battle in France at least 31 chaplains were in German captivity.

New Corps

After Dunkirk the British Army began to rebuild shattered forces and replace lost equipment and, though there was no immediate need to reorganize the existing Corps, changes were made to fill gaps revealed by nine months of war. The first was the creation of the Intelligence Corps in July 1940. Before the war regimental officers had been given short courses to educate them for intelligence duties in the battalion or brigade, but it was only in September 1939 that the War Office Directorate of Military Intelligence created a School for Intelligence Training to provide intensive tuition for selected individuals. On mobilization an Intelligence force for the BEF assembled at Aldershot; the officers remained in their regiments and the Field Security Section soldiers were badged as Military Police. This intelligence system operated without suffering any embarrassments as serious as the 'Venlo Incident', in which two Secret Intelligence Service (SIS or MI6) representatives were lured to the Dutch border town and kidnapped by German agents on 9 November 1939. However, military intelligence duties expanded so rapidly that strict control of operations and personnel proved impossible without a central staff. The motto of the new Corps was *Manui Dat Cognitio Vires* (Knowledge Gives Strength to the Arm). Accurate intelligence information was to be essential to the success of future Allied commanders, and this was abundantly supplied by the new Corps and the Army's Special Wireless Sections, which had only appointed the first German-speaking Intelligence Officer to a field 'Y' section in early spring 1940.

The second change was designed to strengthen the Army in a literal sense. The Army Physical Training Corps was formed from the Army Physical Training Staff, which had been rapidly run down from a strength of 2,299 in 1919 to only 150 in 1922, and continued to be undermanned, though by 1935 serious concern was being expressed about the general decline in the physical standards of recruits. At the outbreak of war the establishment had only increased to 280, totally inadequate for the huge task ahead, so men with civil physical training qualifications - schoolmasters, sports coaches, and sportsmen - were recruited to make up the numbers. Meanwhile the Swedish system of gymnastic development of the whole body was modified with more practical exercises in 'lifting and handling' and 'gun manhandling' to meet the requirements of modern warfare. In September 1940 the Staff was formed into a combatant Corps; all instructors received weapons training and began to wear uniform to emphasise the link between training and the reality of warfare. These changes brought the new Corps into line with the other technical experts of the British Army, who were also professional soldiers. During the battle in France, many Corps officers and soldiers had unhesitatingly abandoned their specialist roles and fought in the line with the infantry. The Army expected nothing less.

Further Reading

Andrew, Christopher *Secret Service* London, Heinemann, 1985

Bidwell, S *The Women's Royal Army Corps* London, Leo Cooper, 1977

Clabby, Brigadier J *The History of the Royal Army Veterinary Corps 1919-1961* London, J A Allen, 1963

Crew, F A E *The Army Medical Services, Vol I Administration* London, HMSO, 1953

Fernyhough, Brigadier A H *History of the Royal Army Ordnance Corps* London, RAOC, not dated

Hawker, Major D S *An Outline of the Early History of the Intelligence Corps* The Rose and the Laurel, Vol 7 No 27, December 1965

History of the Royal Army Dental Corps Aldershot, RADC, 1971

Kennett, Brigadier B B and Tatman, Colonel J A *Craftsmen of the Army, the Story of REME* London, Leo Cooper, 1970

Lovell-Knight, Major A V *The Story of the Royal Military Police* London, Leo Cooper, 1977

Nalder, Major-General R F H *The History of British Army Signals in the Second World War* London, Royal Signals Institution, 1953

Oldfield, Lieutenant-Colonel E A L *History of the Army Physical Training Corps* Aldershot, Gale and Polden, 1955

Pakenham-Walsh, Major-General R P *History of the Corps of Royal Engineers* Chatham, Institution of Royal Engineers, 1958

Rhodes-Wood, Major E H *A War History of the Royal Pioneer Corps 1939-1945* London, Gale and Polden, 1960

Skillen, Hugh *Spies of the Airwaves* Privately published, 1989

Smyth, Brigadier Sir John *In This Sign Conquer* London, A R Mowbray, 1968

The Story of the Royal Army Service Corps 1939-1945 London, G Bell, 1955

White, Colonel A C T *The Story of Army Education 1643-1963* London, Harrap, 1963

'How Is The Empire?'

'Both with gratitude for the past, and with confidence in the future, we arrange ourselves without fear beside Britain. Where she goes, we go, where she stands, we stand.'

With these brave words, New Zealand's Prime Minister Michael Joseph Savage brought his country into the Second World War. In September 1939 as in August 1914 the British Commonwealth and Empire followed the mother country with enthusiasm and loyalty into a European conflict. After just seven months of the war, one-sixth of all male Australians between the ages of 20 and 29 had volunteered for war against a distant, inactive foe. Indeed, the response throughout the Empire was such as to justify the Hoare Committee's confident recommendation made on 8 September that four of the fifty-five divisions to be raised and equipped over the following two years could be supplied by the Indian Army and at least fourteen further divisions could be composed of men from the dominions, where ties of blood remained, apparently, as strong as ever.

> **66** *At such a moment as this the assurances of support that we have received from the Empire are a source of profound encouragement to us* **99**
> *Neville Chamberlain,*
> *3 September 1939*

But on closer inspection there were significant differences between 1914 and 1939. While the Governments of Australia and New Zealand both declared war on 3 September, as soon as they heard of Britain's action, both insisted that their forces should stand apart as national units, not distributed throughout the British Army. The Canadian Government would not act until its parliament reassembled, declaring war only on 10 September. Two days earlier, the Canadian Premier, Mackenzie King, promised that he would never impose conscription, an attitude shared by Robert Menzies who guaranteed Australians that overseas service would not be made compulsory. And although South Africa waited only three days, this short interval concealed considerable political strife, the Prime Minister General Hertzog wishing to remain neutral, being refused a dissolution by the Governor-General, and being replaced by General Smuts who led his country into war. He too refused to consider enforced military service outside South Africa, although in March 1940 most members of the Union Defence Force swore a voluntary oath to serve 'anywhere in Africa'. The 'new' dominion, Ireland, refused to side with Britain and remained neutral throughout the war.

The Empire's colonies, of course, had no choice but to join in Britain's fight. Most did so with a will, established local defence forces from Malta to Hong Kong, from Burma to Fiji, recruiting and training against probable and improbable attacks. In far-off Fiji, for example, the declaration of war was followed by a mobilization and a three-day camp from 7 to 9 September from which it was possible to gazette eleven units, including a Force HQ and Signals, Labour, Transport, and Supply Companies, two infantry companies and a medical section. Even in India, which had moved some way down the road towards self-government with the administrative reforms of the 1930s, the Viceroy Lord Linlithgow declared war without reference to Congress, the leading nationalist party, or, for that matter, to anyone else: Britain's decision bound India as firmly as any shire county. His decision was, by and large, accepted, for fascism was seen as the enemy of aspiring as well as established democracies, but Congress nevertheless issued a statement maintaining that 'if co-operation is desired in a worthy cause, this cannot be obtained by compulsion and imposition'.

An Empire Unprepared

Restrictions on the role which a number of these Imperial forces could play were imposed as much by practicalities as by politics and national aspirations. The dominions were no better geared for modern war than was Britain, and the logistical preparation of troops inevitably took time, however great the will to fight. In New Zealand, enlistment began on 12 September and within four weeks nearly 15,000 men had applied. But the first 6,000 troops did not sail for Egypt until January 1940, and the second *echelon* departed only on 2 May. Australia, alarmed at the threat that was Japan, agreed in mid-September to raise one division with auxiliaries for home or foreign service 'as circumstances permit', and two drafts of the militia, each 40,000 strong, were called up for one month's training. Recruitment for Australia's 6th Division was slow: of the 80,000 militiamen called up for training, fewer than 5,000 volunteered to serve in the Expeditionary Force - less than half the figure the government had anticipated - and of 100,000 Australians who volunteered for service overseas against Germany by the end of March, only 22% were in the Army, while 68% had applied to join the Air Force.

Earmarked for service overseas, the first troops from Canada's 1st Division left Halifax by boat in December 1939, arriving in Britain to an enthusiastic reception from the British and French press. But its third 'flight' did not depart until the end of January 1940, one not-insignificant cause of the delay being some reluctance from the Canadian government to supply specialist troops requested by Britain. Recruitment for a second division to serve abroad was slow before the crisis of May 1940. On the outbreak of war, it was agreed with the War Office that Newfoundlanders should be enlisted for the Royal Artillery, but the first draft of 403 volunteers from that loyal but thinly-populated land did not leave for Britain until April 1940.

The Strength of India

Including non-combatants, the Indian Army in October 1939 was 194,000 strong, with Frontier, Irregular, Auxiliary, and State forces totalling another 100,000 men: a vast pool of potential manpower waiting to be tapped. On 4 September 1939, the Chatfield Report was published, which considered the role which India might play in a global war. It recommended that the Army in India should include a specifically External Defence Force, better trained and equipped than troops intended purely for the defence of India itself. In fact, this proposal had been anticipated by necessity: the Indian Army's role had been debated for many years, and with the old threat from Russia declining by the 1930s attention had turned more and more to its potential to supply troops for Imperial defence. Some steps had been

Armoured car *Renown* and its crew, Wana Column on the Tanai-Gulkach road, India, North-West Frontier 1936. From a photograph album compiled by Colonel G F M Stray MC National Army Museum 7810-14-27

taken towards modernization of an Army alleged in a 1938 report to be falling behind the standards of the Egyptian, Iraqi, and Afghan forces, and even by 1936 external commitments included two brigades for Egypt, a brigade each for Singapore, Burma, the Persian Gulf and the Red Sea. Some 60% of the troops marked out by the Chatfield Committee as suitable for the External Defence Force, including 11th Indian Brigade Group, had embarked for service overseas, and on 7 September the rest of the projected force was told to prepare for the journey to Egypt, where the two brigades were grouped into the 4th Division. But the Indian Army too suffered from problems of supply and equipment. India's economy was scarcely geared to provide armaments, and Britain could neither spare any of her own insufficient production nor supply sufficient dollars to purchase equipment from the United States.

Lanchester armoured cars of the 12th Royal Lancers, Egypt c1934
National Army Museum 7711-159-117

To May 1940, the Empire's armies could only await Hitler's next move. This was not conducive to improve morale, neither was it designed to enhance the popularity of governments at home. In South Africa, the Afrikaaner Nationalists tried to carry a resolution in parliament that war with Germany should be ended forthwith. Although the Smuts Government won the day, comparisons were voiced with Ireland, 'which also was a British Dominion, but which has broken the fetters', comparisons which were hard to forget. The lack of action also doubtless adversely affected recruiting: in Australia, after the departure of 6th Division for Egypt, only 811

men volunteered for service in the Army overseas in January, and 217 in February. Once the formation of 7th Division had been announced on 28 February, 6,757 enlisted during March and April. But the administrative machine moved slowly, as administrative machines will, and no commanders of the new division, and of the Army Corps that the two divisions would constitute, were appointed for another five weeks.

Responding to Crisis

The collapse of the allied armies in western Europe during May and June 1940 was the stimulus to British demands for stronger support from her Empire. On 16 June 1940, Churchill explained to all prime ministers of the dominions that Britain was resolved to continue the struggle, not through blind obstinacy but because of an appreciation of 'the real strength of our position' - a strength drawn from her own spirit and resources, but equally from those of her dominions and colonies. Again, though, the response was mixed. Canada, Australia, and New Zealand all promised to stand by the mother country. Canada, for example, stepped up the preparation of a second overseas division, and pressed ahead with raising 3rd and 4th Divisions, a Canadian Army Corps finally being formed on Christmas Day 1940. In Australia, Menzies called for 'all-round sacrifice, unremitting toil and unflinching devotion' at this hour of peril, and whereas 8,000 had been accepted for the Army in May 1940, the June figure was 48,500, sufficient manpower not only for 7th Division, but for three more divisions. Yet old problems could not be concealed. On 11 July Australia's War Cabinet felt compelled to suspend recruitment for the Army, the reasons being the loss of men from vital industrial occupations, depletion of militia strength, and that perennial difficulty: lack of equipment.

In October [1939] the Regiment marched the 150 miles to Rawalpindi, and the next month paraded for the last time as a horsed cavalry regiment ... The horses were handed over to various Indian State Forces, many to Jodpur and Patiala, and things could never be the same again but for himmat i mardan madad i khudda which ... means 'by the courage of men and with the help of God' Edward George Haynes, *The Last Days of Horsed Cavalry: An Account of Skinner's Horse Between the Wars*
National Army Museum 8711-55: Photo 7710-9

Hertzog again tried to move the South African Parliament into making peace with Germany and Italy, which had broken its neutrality on 10 June. Describing England as 'a fugitive from the continent of Europe, defeated and threatened', he forced a vote on the motion which, though defeated, showed a weakening in the Government's support. India too looked on askance. Nehru, leader of Congress, opposed active support for either side, seeing no reason for Indians to prop up 'tottering Imperialism', but urging that nationalist forces ought not to take advantage of Britain's weakness. Nehru could not speak for all India, though, and the loyal Indian Army remained a great source of strength throughout the war years.

The Burden of Empire

Of course, the concept of Imperial Commitment carried obligations along with benefits. So far, we have considered the Empire as a source of military strength, despite the conditions and restrictions which limited the Chiefs-of-Staff's scope of action. But the Empire also required a British commitment to garrison and operational duties. Throughout the 1930s about one half of the British Army's total strength was deployed in garrisons throughout the world.

Thus at the end of 1937 there were 106,704 men, including 64 infantry battalions, stationed in the United Kingdom, but at the same time there were over 90,000 overseas: 53,951 in 45 infantry battalions comprising the British garrison in India, 18 battalions and 21,187 men in the Middle East and Mediterranean, a battalion and 1,800 men in the West Indies - the West India Regiment having been disbanded in 1927 - and 8 battalions with 12,143 men stationed in the Far East. From 1st Bn The East Surrey Regiment in the Sudan to 1st Bn The Sherwood Foresters in Jamaica, from 2nd Bn The Highland Light Infantry in Peshawar to 1st Bn The Lancashire Fusiliers in Tientsin, British forces garrisoned the globe. Civil unrest in both India and Palestine had led to increased military commitments during the 1930s. The position in Palestine, a mandated territory from the First World War, was particularly immediate: during the 1920s the RAF had been detailed to provide the police there with military support, just as they had done successfully in Iraq. But the RAF's resources for this task were ludicrously inadequate, and in any case reprisal bombing raids on villages, a tactic that had worked in Iraq, could hardly be expected to be effective in populous, urban Palestine. By 1938, 7th and 8th Divisions were deployed in the country, facing an increasingly difficult task.

Men of the Lancashire Fusiliers with a field gun, armoured car in background, China c1937
National Army Museum 7605-68-77

Britain, like Australia, looked with concern upon the rising menace of the Japanese Empire. While Japan had stated that she intended to remain 'independent' in the war, she had made strong 'recommendations' that the American and European governments withdraw their fleets and troops from parts of China then under her control. The probability was that Japan's involvement in China would keep her fully occupied in the immediate future, but she was clearly an unpredictable force in the Far East which could not be disregarded. The defence of Singapore accounted for most of the British and Indian troops stationed east of Suez: two brigades, one British, one Indian, were in Malaya. Further east, there was a predominantly-British infantry Brigade and an Indian infantry battalion in Hong Kong, and a British infantry brigade was responsible for garrisoning the Chinese treaty ports of Shanghai and Tientsin. In the event of war, these isolated troops could hardly be supported, but political considerations dictated that they stay.

Britain was not without plans for her Army's imperial role in the event of war. Securing the Suez Canal against a possible threat from Italy had long been at the heart of British strategic thinking. Canadians apart, the Commonwealth and Indian forces were concentrated in Egypt when war came, augmenting the British forces already there, but assumptions that Italy would side with Germany and so provide a target for military campaigns against her colonies in North and East Africa were frustrated by Mussolini's reluctance to declare war. In August 1939 the highly-respected General Sir Archibald Wavell was moved from Southern Command to become General Officer Commanding-in-Chief, Middle East, with instructions to form a joint staff with naval and RAF commanders for planning purposes. His land forces on appointment consisted of an armoured division - then still being assembled and later to be designated the 7th Armoured Division - and three British infantry brigades with artillery and engineer support. He also had at his disposal 11th Indian Brigade Group and local defence forces such as the Jordanian Arab Legion, which gave sterling service, garrisoning strategically-vital points throughout the Middle East. Having supplied one brigade to Egypt, Palestine retained three infantry brigades along with supporting troops. Two British battalions were then stationed in the Sudan, and there were small garrisons in Gibraltar and Malta.

Curiously, it was Italy's entrance into the war that gave the Imperial strategists the chance they had been waiting for. Egypt was at once reinforced with a large proportion of Britain's remaining Class I tank strength, and these forces spearheaded the successful campaigns by Empire troops in late 1940 and early 1941.

An Alliance of Empires

There is a final aspect of Imperial commitment that should not be forgotten, since it affected and stimulated planning for the colonial forces. Before the fall of France, Britain was a partner in an alliance of Empires. France's colonies also contributed significantly to her war effort: of the twenty-eight infantry divisions maintained by France in the 1930s, eight were North African or colonial divisions stationed in the homeland, and in 1939 the 120,000-strong Army in Syria and Lebanon stood as a strategic reserve against Italian ambitions. In August 1939 the French Government asked Britain for plans to recruit more men from African colonies south of the Sahara. The War Office responded by stepping up recruitment in these colonies, ostensibly aiming to double numerical strength, while the Colonial Office set about considering the best use to be made of colonial manpower. It was concluded, however, that for two years at least 'the raising of new combatant units in the Colonial Dependencies will not on strict military merits be practicable' - there were no resources available to equip them. Local defence and pioneer units were considered to be the only roles for colonial troops, and even the five brigades of the King's African Rifles and Royal West African Frontier Force were not equipped

to the standard required for 'secondary' theatres of the war. That said, 1st and 2nd (later 11th and 12th) African Divisions, a combination of East and West African brigades, were sufficiently prepared by late 1940 to play a decisive role in the conquest of Italian East Africa.

Further Reading

Barclay, G St J The Empire is Marching London, Wiedenfeld and Nicolson, 1976

Connell, John Wavell: Scholar and Soldier London, Collins, 1964

Howlett, R A (ed) The History of the Fiji Military Forces 1939-1945 1948

King, Michael New Zealanders at War Auckland, Heinemann, 1981

Long, Gavin The Six Years War, Australia in the 1939-45 War Canberra, 1973

Mason, P A Matter of Honour Harmondsworth, Peregrine Books, 1976

Orpen, Neil South African Forces in World War II : East African and Abyssinian Campaigns Cape Town, 1968

Perry, F W The Commonwealth Armies, Manpower and Organization in Two World Wars Manchester University Press, 1988

Prasad, Sri Nandan Expansion of the Armed Forces and Defence Organisation Delhi, Combined Historical Section, 1956

Stacey, C P Six Years of War Ottawa, 1955

'The Readiness is All'

On the evening of 1 September 1939, Neville Chamberlain addressed a packed and sombre House of Commons. With all hope of peace now virtually extinct he looked back to the summer of 1914, drawing a favourable comparison with the situation at the outbreak of the First World War. Pointing to Government preparations over the preceding months the Prime Minister noted that civil defence plans were far advanced, that military forces were up to strength, indeed, that 'all three Services are ready' for the struggle ahead.

But how far, in reality, did this state of readiness extend? It had been accepted since 1935 that the Territorial Army would bear the Army's share of protecting the homeland, a decision that produced what a contemporary publication described with some justification as a 'military revolution' in the Territorial Army, hitherto intended as a supplementary field force, but hereafter detailed to provide troops for Anti-Aircraft (AA) and Coastal Defence duties as well. By March 1939, more than 40% of the TA's strength fulfilled these defensive roles, with 75,000 men serving in AA units and 8,000 manning the 9.2-inch guns and other fortifications on the south and east coasts. But as we shall see, the TA was deficient both in manpower and - crucially - in up-to-date equipment. If catastrophe were to overtake the allies on the continent, could much be expected of those left behind?

> 66 *Guns and searchlights are spread in a wide chequer-board over the land, by lonely copses, along farm buildings, in the hills, in the Fen country, keeping an increasing watch over our homes day and night* 99
>
> *Hore-Belisha, speech at inaugural dinner of London Welsh Regiment 18 July 1939*

Anti-Aircraft

Under operational control of the Air Ministry, the Territorial Army's newly-reorganized Anti-Aircraft Command was central to plans for home defence. As late as 1922 the Army had been responsible for searchlights and Anti-Aircraft guns, and even after the RAF had taken over control of air defence the Army continued to man ground weaponry and equipment. But for many years little was done to fulfil these obligations, and it was only after two major reports on the state of air defence in the mid-1930s, the Brooke-Popham Committee Report of 1935 and the Dowding Report of 1937, that real progress began to be made. Both criticised the current state of anti-aircraft defences, rendered obsolete by the development of radar coupled with the growing sophistication of long-range bombers, and both wished to see such defences developed away from the coast and extended up the east coast to the Forth-Clyde line. The Dowding Report recommended provision of at least 158 coastal AA batteries, together with a minimum of 196 searchlight companies. But these figures, while accepted as no more than was necessary, called for at least 50,000 more men and a great deal of new weaponry. Neither was readily available.

An Army Short of Men

It was a problem that could be and would be overcome with the outbreak of war, but the

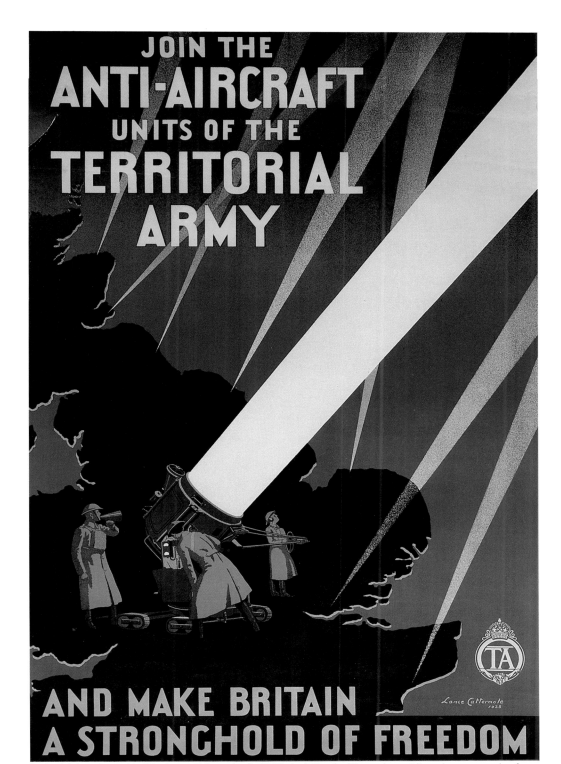

Territorial Army Poster No 3 by Lance Cattermole, (b.1898) depicting the TA carrying out its main pre-war role of home defence
National Army Museum 8401-55

Two soldiers of the 3rd County of London Yeomanry, in a light tank, wielding a shotgun. The Sharpshooters were stationed in the United Kingdom until August 1941
National Army Museum 7503-63-1

shortage of manpower nevertheless lingered on into the winter of 1939. Early that April there were five existing and two projected divisions in the TA's Anti-Aircraft Command, the result of several conversions of infantry battalions to anti-aircraft units in the late-1930s. The first anti-aircraft divisions of the TA had been formed in January 1936 - principally from south-eastern units such as 7th Battalion Essex Regiment, 6th City of London (City of London Rifles) and 7th City of London (Post Office Rifles) - and by the end of 1938 two divisions were employed on air-defence duties along the east coast of Britain. The two divisions were then, however, at only 60% of their 48,000-man establishment, and Hore-Belisha, at first an advocate of the expansion of Territorial air defence, had begun to realise that a full commitment of this nature must prove a serious drain on limited manpower increasingly required elsewhere. The lack of men showed up on mobilization in September 1939, many Territorial battalions having failed to duplicate in time. 7th Battalion The Worcestershire Regiment, for example, consisted of just 380 men at the end of

September, and in November it was felt necessary to create general-service battalions from companies of the National Defence Corps.

Formed in 1936 and affiliated to the TA, the National Defence Corps was one of several reserve formations assisting in the duties of home defence. It was made up of men between the ages of 45 and 55 who had previous service experience and was designed to supply guard detachments. The Regular Reserve of men who had completed their six- or seven-year colours service was augmented by a Supplementary Reserve in existence since 1924. This body existed to supply the specialist requirements of some arms, training running for at most a fortnight each year. To this, a 17,000-strong infantry section had been added in 1936. In September 1938 the Auxiliary Territorial Service was formed, offering women over the age of eighteen the chance to enlist either for Local or more General Service. Nor should one forget the expansion of the Observer Corps in 1937, which materially assisted searchlight crews with reporting and spotting duties.

Pre-war thinking worked on the assumption that the enemy would attempt a 'knock-out blow' on strategic points within hours of the outbreak of hostilities. Preparedness was thus the watchword, and both during the Munich Crisis of September 1938 and in the slide towards war one year later the smooth - if often improvised - mobilization of forces was impressive. From all the available sources, over 546,000 Territorials and Reservists were mobilized in August-September 1939: The Government had ordered the permanent manning of certain anti-aircraft defences - the 'couverture' of 288 guns and 960 searchlights - from the end of May, which involved the call-out of the Territorial AA units in four contingents for a month at a time. Some additional Territorial units were mobilized on 21 August to man anti-aircraft and important coastal defences. National Defence Companies were called-out four days later, with both Regular and Supplementary reserves being mobilized on the last day of the month. Finally, the invasion of Poland marked the embodiment of the 29 Yeomanry regiments, 12 tank, and 232 infantry battalions of the TA.

Finding manpower was one thing, finding manpower of the right calibre was quite another. For most new recruits the Army was not the first choice. Those with skills, especially, looked elsewhere, which was worrying given that the Army's requirements had altered since the First World War. Official figures showed that the proportion of infantrymen in the Army of 1939 was only one-third that of 1914. The mechanized Army's need for more skilled men lost out both to the labour force withheld by 'reserved occupations' and to the equally-pressing needs for skills in the more-attractive Royal Navy and RAF.

The position with regard to home defence was worse still, for the troops allocated to such duties were often those rejected for one reason or another by the Field Force and the specialist corps. While impressed by and grateful for the high calibre of most of his men, General Sir Frederick Pile, Commander-in-Chief Anti-Aircraft Command, noted the problems caused by the sudden influx in October of 11,000 resentful 'immatures', sent back from BEF TA Divisions because they were under age for service overseas, and he observed, too, that of the twenty-five militiamen arriving at a 'fairly representative battery' just before Christmas 1939, 'one had a withered arm, one was mentally deficient, one had no thumbs', and 'one had a glass eye which fell out whenever he doubled to the guns'. Of some 1,000 recruits in 31st AA Brigade, he considered as many as 10% to have been either physically or psychologically unsuitable, even considered against an undemanding standard.

A Modern Army?

But manpower problems were as nothing compared with the shortfalls in adequate equipment and modern weapons. British industry was not geared to supply a large army; the factories simply were not ready. The problem had been compounded by the Royal Navy's decision, in the Spring of 1939, to use both Rosyth and Scapa Flow as bases for the Home Fleet in the event of war. The protection of Naval support vessels thus assumed a greater importance than ever, twenty-four heavy AA guns being required for Scapa Flow, three times the previous estimate. With serious delays in the supply of AA weaponry, defences still relied on the largely-obsolete three-inch gun. The first of the much-needed 4.5-inch guns was brought into service only in February 1939, and whereas the Army requirement for the new 3.7-inch gun in June 1939 had been estimated at 1,300, by the end of September only some

Sergeant Percy Stanford, of the 5th Sussex (Worthing) Bn, Home Guard in 1940, painted by Lance Cattermole. Stanford wears battledress denims and holds an American P14 rifle.
National Army Museum 8403-54

'AGAINST ALL ODDS'

thirty were in service. Figures for the Bofors gun were little better, about 13% of estimated requirements being available by the first month of war, some of these having been purchased from potentially-vulnerable factories in Poland, Belgium, and Hungary. Ammunition, too, was often outdated. With priority being given to the needs of the Army in France, troops left behind lacked even basic equipment. As General Pile wrote later, his own command had become 'the residuary legatees of a fast-diminishing estate'.

The Army also supplied the men who would combat any incursion on the ground. In November 1939, land forces under General Sir Walter Kirke, Commander-in-Chief Home Forces, amounted to nine infantry divisions, components of three others, a cavalry division, an armoured division, and an armoured brigade, grouped into five regional commands. The General had at his disposal twenty-five cruiser and 267 light tanks. With mobilization, the training function of Regular units stationed in Britain came to an end and a replacement system became an urgent priority. Infantry regimental depots became training centres, and holding battalions were created to take men from these camps and begin further training on a sub-unit level. Seven Training Regiments were formed in September 1939. The training of troops began throughout the country, and whilst in training all these forces could be used, in an emergency, to supplement the needs of home defence. They were a constant, if constantly changing, reservoir on which the planners could draw.

A Winter Spent in Waiting

Until the spring of 1940, training and planning, often in extremely uncomfortable conditions, were indeed the orders of the day, for anti-aircraft crews, for reservists, and for those destined for Finland, France, or Egypt alike. Apart from raids on the Firth of Forth and Scapa Flow from October 1939, German air activity was minimal. As the remorselessly-cold winter of 1939-40 began to bite, transport bringing supplies to isolated coastal AA outposts in Norfolk and Lincolnshire took to the fields in order to avoid fifteen-foot snow drifts, and whole units camped out in tents through the worst of the winter because of inadequate provision for permanent shelter. There was not a lot of time in which to feel cold, though. As Colonel Sir Thomas Butler, then Assistant Adjutant at the Guards Depot at Caterham, recalled, men were 'really too busy, we were really flat out doing our duties . . . we didn't get much sleep in those days'. AA crews - including the first mixed male-and-female crew which began initial training early in 1940 - suffered from lack of practice, since even in established practice camps the shortages extended to towing and target-aircraft. The fortunate men trained in the new drill halls erected during the building programme of the late-1930s, but for many, perhaps a majority, the old volunteer drill halls had to suffice, and even an official TA recruiting booklet of 1939 admitted that 'the improvised use of village halls which served well enough for the volunteers when Napoleon threatened, does not meet the needs of a 3.7-inch battery'.

Before the outbreak of war invasion seemed highly unlikely, yet after a few weeks of German naval activity in home waters the possibility of small raids or even a more substantial invasion began to seem less remote. The Chiefs of Staff took the view, however, that none of the field formations then in training and intended for other duties should be transferred to counter this threat. They advised that as many troops as 'suitable' should be stationed near the east coast while based in the country, and that these forces should be so organized that they could be concentrated swiftly in reaction to an alarm given by special air and sea reconnaissance. The immediate response to the mining of coastal waters, however, was restricted to increased air and sea patrols and the creation of the Nore Flotilla - three paddle steamers, each armed with a Bofors and a pair of searchlights, and manned by an AA Command regiment - which spotlighted intruders, destroyed numerous floating mines, and rescued the survivors from ships which came to grief in the Thames Estuary during the first half of 1940.

Julius Caesar

The recommendations of the Chiefs of Staff formed the basis of the so-called *Julius Caesar* plan, the heart of home defence thinking until the German onslaught of May 1940. With no knock-out blow having been attempted, the

BACK THEM UP!

'Back Them Up!' by Terence Cuneo (b.1907), a Government poster published in 1940 when Britain stood alone in German-dominated Europe

plan started from the belief that in any sizeable operation the Germans would target a port. It assumed also, not unnaturally, that the most likely scenario would be a combined amphibious and air operation. When studying this hypothetical threat, General Kirke reasoned that if air support could be eliminated at an early stage such an invasion would surely fail. Accordingly, he concentrated his plans on destroying parachute and other airborne forces as they landed. The concern that ports might be assaulted from land as well as sea was emphasized by orders to Southern, Northern, and Eastern Commands to provide infantry for the defence of port perimeters. Naturally, the plan relied heavily on efficient co-operation with the Navy and RAF. Were an enemy force to land, two bomber squadrons, an Army Co-operation squadron, and communication aircraft would give Home Command direct support, and a bomber force was on standby to attack German naval targets as opportunity arose, with all bombers in Britain naturally available to attack a hostile armada.

Julius Caesar also considered the need to control the civil population in threatened areas. Evacuation, never a favourite option in view of the adverse affect on morale, was opposed as it had been in 1914, but by encouraging civilians to stay put the authorities had to accept that they might have a nuisance value in the event of invasion, hindering the free movement of troops and supplies. Plans were accordingly drawn up to withdraw civilians in the most exposed areas by routes which avoided the main supply roads.

It was perhaps as well that the paper plans were never put to the test. Kirke estimated that he would need a minimum of seven properly-equipped divisions for *Julius Caesar*, one each in Northern and Scottish Commands, two in the most vulnerable Eastern Command Area, and three in reserve. On 1 May 1940 he had nine divisions available, but the supplying of a third Corps to France, of troops to Norway, and the loss of 1st Cavalry Division to the Middle East robbed his force of much of its experience and 'muscle'. 1st Armoured Division, moreover, was in HQ Reserve in Southern Command ready to leave for France. The weak 9th Division was spread over the entire Scottish coastline, the still-embryonic 2nd Armoured Division held responsibility for a large part of Northern Command's operational area, and three training divisions - 43rd, 45th, and 52nd - formed a major element in Southern Command. 1st Canadian Division which had arrived in January provided welcome reinforcement for the troops of 1st London, 55th, and 18th Divisions, the front line of Eastern Command. Four divisions allocated for aid to the civil power - 2nd London, 38th, 59th, and 61st - were stationed in the conurbations of Greater London, South Wales, South Lancashire, and the Midlands respectively.

The Prime Minister told Parliament that the British Army was ready for war; Adolf Hitler declared to the Reichstag at the same time that he was fully 'aware of the greatness of this hour'. Preparedness on paper was one thing, awareness of an opportunity quite another. It was partly as a result of this different emphasis that Germany's great gamble of May 1940 succeeded. Equally, it was as well that her gambling had limits, and that the vulnerability of troops left behind in Britain was not exposed prematurely to the shock of war.

Further Reading

Collier, Basil *The Defence of the United Kingdom* London, HMSO, 1957

Dennis, Peter *The Territorial Army 1907-1940* London, The Royal Historical Society, 1987

Gibbs, N H *Grand Strategy Vol I* London, HMSO, 1976

JK (Colonel J K Dunlop) *The Territorial Army Today* London, Adam and Charles Black, 1939

Liddell Hart, Basil *The Defence of Britain* London, Faber and Faber, 1939

Minney, R J *The Private Papers of Hore-Belisha* London, Collins, 1960

Pile, General Sir Frederick *Ack-Ack* London, Harrap, 1949

Roof Over Britain : The Official Story of Britain's Anti-Aircraft Defences 1939-1942 London, HMSO, 1943

63

'AGAINST ALL ODDS'

In the Autumn of 1939, for the second time this century, a British Expeditionary Force (BEF) sailed to France to fight a land war against Germany and her allies. Yet the decision to commit part of Britain's limited military resources to the organization of an Expeditionary Force for action in Europe had been taken only some seven months before war was declared. Thus when, a little over a year later, the Army was called upon to repulse the German *Blitzkrieg* (lightning war), it is hardly surprising that it was found in many respects to be ill-trained, ill-equipped, and psychologically unprepared for the task. The roots of the Army's manpower and equipment problems are discussed elsewhere in this publication, but it is against a background of neglect and shortage that the story of the Army in the campaigns of 1940 must be considered.

> 66 *I go so far as to say that if we come through the winter without any large or important event occurring we shall in fact have gained the first campaign of the war* 99
>
> *Churchill, 12 November 1939*

'The Mother of the British Army'

In the years immediately before 1939, the opinion was widely held that the opening campaign of the Second World War would be fought from trenches similar to those which had dominated the conflict of 1914-18. This static warfare would, it was believed, allow the British a period of grace in which to build up the Army before the time was ripe to take the offensive. The months between September 1939 and May 1940, a period which became popularly known as the 'Phoney War', did indeed provide a brief respite, and the BEF which, in General Sir Edmund Ironside's view, had now become 'the mother of the British Army' landed in France prepared less to fight a war, than to train for one.

The German re-occupation of the Rhineland in 1936 had persuaded the British and French to begin an exchange of military information, but it was only with the worsening international climate after the Munich crisis in 1938 that formal, and secret, staff talks began. During these talks, the first of which was held in London at the end of March 1939, any lingering hopes the French might have entertained that the BEF would be either significant in size or speedy in its arrival were finally dashed. The French delegates were informed that the Expeditionary Force would comprise four Regular infantry divisions which would take the field within thirty-three days of mobilization, and that thereafter, reinforcements would probably arrive at the rate of two Territorial divisions within four months, and four more divisions within six months. It was unlikely that an armoured division would be deployed in France earlier than eight months after mobilization.

This news did nothing to encourage the French to abandon their essentially-defensive strategy, or to risk their troops beyond the apparent security of the Maginot Line in pre-emptive attacks on the German frontier. The defence of France was to be the immediate objective of the Allies. It was believed that this could be accomplished by imposing an economic blockade on Germany, and by conducting psychological warfare aimed at persuading the Germans to disown their leaders. If an enemy offensive was launched its impetus would be absorbed by fixed defences, and a counter-attack mounted once Allied resources were equal to the task. The BEF was to form part

'AGAINST ALL ODDS'

of the French North-East Theatre of Operations, opposite the Belgian frontier, with a French Army on either flank. On the day that war was declared it was at last given a Commander-in-Chief in the person of General Viscount Gort VC, who since 1937 had been Chief of the Imperial General Staff, the professional head of the Army. In turn Gort was responsible to the British Government as the C-in-C of all British troops in France, and also, since the conduct of land operations was in the hands of the French, to his immediate field commander, the French General Georges.

Initially, Gort's Command embraced a general headquarters and two army corps each of two divisions, plus support troops. I Corps (1st and 2nd Divisions) was commanded by Lieutenant-General Sir John Dill, and II Corps (3rd and 4th Divisions) by Lieutenant-General Alan Brooke.

The combat elements of the BEF were:

43	Infantry Battalions
4	Machine Gun Battalions
2	Cavalry Regiments (light AFVs)
1	Army Tank Battalion
20	Field Artillery Regiments
1	Heavy Artillery Regiment
7	Medium Artillery Regiments Supporting Anti-Aircraft and Anti-Tank Units

In three-and-a-half weeks, between 9 September and 4 October 1939 the first *echelon* of the BEF, comprising some 160,000 men, 25,000 vehicles, and 140,000 tons of stores, was convoyed to France without loss. By 12 October the BEF had taken over twenty-five miles of the front line in the Lille sector, but few,

if any, of its units were as yet fully equipped for war. Most alarming of all, Gort's four divisions had stepped into an arena in which they were dwarfed by the other combatants. At the beginning of September 1939, for example, the French were preparing to deploy some 80 divisions, while the Germans could call upon 105 field divisions.

Fortunately, the seven months from October 1939 to May 1940 allowed time for reinforcement and preparation for battle. The 5th Infantry Division, consisting of Regulars, arrived in December, to be followed in January by the first Territorial division, 48th (South Midland) to be deployed in France. The 50th (Northumbrian) Division and the 51st (Highland) Division followed in February, with two further Territorial divisions, 42nd (East Lancashire) and 44th (Home Counties), landing in April. It was now possible to field a third Army Corps under Lieutenant-General Sir Ronald Adam consisting of Territorial divisions. Of the BEF's strength of 394,165 officers and men, 237,319 were available for combat organized as a GHQ Reserve and five Regular and five Territorial infantry divisions. The divisions were grouped as follows:

I Corps Lieutenant-General M Barker
1st, 2nd, 48th Divisions

II Corps Lieutenant-General A Brooke
3rd, 4th, 5th, 50th Divisions

III Corps Lieutenant-General Sir Ronald Adam
42nd, 44th Divisions

The 51st (Highland) Division had been dispatched to the Saar to gain experience under French command, and three minimally-equipped and only partially-trained Territorial

65

divisions, 12th (Eastern), 23rd (Northumbrian), and 46th (Midland and West Riding), were employed on labour duties.

Norway

While the BEF was awaiting the test of battle in France a new front was opening to the north in Scandinavia. The Allies had been considering military assistance to Finland since that country had been attacked by the Soviet Union in November 1939, but before an Expeditionary Force of British and French troops (FORCE AVONMOUTH), under the command of Major-General P J Mackesy, could sail from the Clyde in March 1940, the Finns concluded an armistice on Russian terms. The 'Winter War' had come to an end, though both the Allies and the Germans remained determined to exploit the strategic resources of Scandinavia, and of the coastal regions of Norway in particular. The Allies, thanks to the preparations for their Finnish

adventure, believed that they were capable of landing a force in Norway which could forestall a German invasion, and hence that Norwegian neutrality could be compromised by mining coastal waters. Hitler and the German Naval Command were, for their part, equally convinced that they must act to prevent any British move to occupy Norway. With ironic precision the combatants planned to put their respective invasion plans into action on the same day, 9 April 1940.

Sightings of major units of the German fleet at sea on 7 and 8 April, however, led the British Admiralty to order its warships to disembark the troops destined for Norway, so that all speed could be made to prevent a German break-out to the Atlantic. In accordance with Operation *Weserübung* (*'Weser'*), on 9 April, German forces occupied Denmark and captured the Norwegian capital, Oslo, together with Trondheim, Bergen, Stavanger, and Narvik.

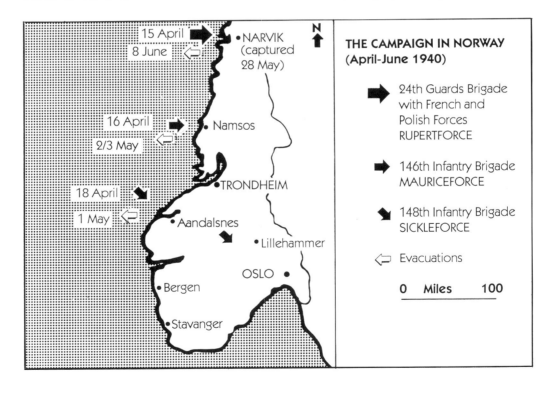

THE CAMPAIGN IN NORWAY
(April–June 1940)

24th Guards Brigade with French and Polish Forces RUPERTFORCE

146th Infantry Brigade MAURICEFORCE

148th Infantry Brigade SICKLEFORCE

Evacuations

0   Miles   100

Having failed to halt the German attack by seapower the Allies turned to the task of counter-invasion. At hand were the troops earmarked for the postponed British landing in Norway, namely eight battalions drawn from the 24th (Guards) Brigade, and the 146th and 148th Territorial Infantry Brigades. Several of these battalions were without vital weapons, ammunition, and radios which had not been unloaded when their transporting warships sailed hurriedly for Norwegian waters. The British force had in any case been equipped for disembarkation at ports which at best could be regarded as friendly and at worst as neutral, and not for opposed landings in arctic conditions. As a result it sailed without armoured fighting vehicles or transport, and with very little artillery.

In the revised British plan, which emerged only after numerous last-minute alterations, RUPERTFORCE (24th Guards Brigade) under Major-General Mackesy was to land at Narvik; SICKLEFORCE (148th Brigade) at first under Brigadier H de R Morgan, and later Major-General B Paget, would land at Aandalsnes; and MAURICEFORCE (146th Brigade) under Major-General Sir Adrian Carton de Wiart was to occupy Namsos. The French contribution to the invasion force included three battalions of *Chasseurs Alpins*, two battalions of the Foreign Legion, and a Polish Brigade recruited in France. Additionally the British raised ten Independent Companies of Territorials of which five were actually deployed.

The Allied operations in Norway centred upon Narvik and, just over 400 miles to the south, the area around Trondheim. Initially, the Regular 15th and Territorial 147th Brigades, plus two battalions of Canadians, were earmarked for an assault landing at Trondheim, but this was cancelled in the face of German air power. Thereafter, an attempt was made to develop the landings at Aandalsnes and Namsos into flanking attacks upon Trondheim, even though the arms of this pincer were held apart by some 200 miles of inhospitable terrain buried deep in snow. The difficulty of this manoeuvre can be appreciated when it is realised that both SICKLEFORCE at Aandalsnes, and MAURICEFORCE at Namsos had been put ashore without any transport or supporting artillery. MAURICEFORCE, pushing south from Namsos was thrown back in some disorder by a German attack which included ski-troops, and evacuation was ordered a week later. At Aandalsnes SICKLEFORCE found itself obliged to tackle German units advancing north from Oslo to link up with their coastal garrisons. Despite co-operation with Norwegian troops and a timely and effective reinforcement by 15th Brigade, it proved impossible to hold a German offensive which could deploy superior firepower and exploit almost-complete mastery of the air. By 2 May SICKLEFORCE had also been evacuated.

The first *echelon* (two companies of 1st Scots Guards) of RUPERTFORCE landed near Sjövegan on the mainland north of Narvik on 14 April, and next day the bulk of the force was put ashore at Harstad, a port on the island of Hinnöy, some thirty-five miles west of Narvik. The attractions of an immediate attack on Narvik were considerable. The German garrison had stood witness to the destruction of its supporting naval force by the Royal Navy, and was thus to all intents and purposes isolated from effective reinforcement, but still the problems of launching a direct assault were felt to be insurmountable. The attacking troops would have to gain a lodgement from open boats through snow several feet deep, in the face of automatic weapons, and probable air attack, and without the benefit of direct naval fire support. Such an attack was judged to be suicidal, and the next three weeks were spent searching for an alternative strategy while tension between the land commander, Major-General Mackesy, and the naval commander, Admiral of the Fleet the Earl of Cork and Orrery, ran high. On 11 May, Lieutenant-General Claude Auchinleck, sent by London to assess the situation, assumed command of the ground forces.

Attempts to destroy the German defences of Narvik by naval bombardment were unsuccessful, and efforts were now concentrated on an overland advance upon the town from north and south. Unfortunately, the strength of RUPERTFORCE was sapped by the need to despatch 24th (Guards) Brigade to the towns of Mo and Bodö, some 200 and 120 miles south of Narvik to block the advance of German forces pushing north. While the Guards conducted a fighting retreat along the coast, Norwegian, French, and Polish troops, supported by ships of the Royal Navy, captured what was left of Narvik on 28 May. However, in the light of the German offensive in France, the decision to withdraw all Allied troops from Norway had already been taken at the end of May.

In effect the Germans had captured Norway, a country larger than the entire British Isles, though with a population of only some three million, in a little under eight weeks using the better part of seven infantry divisions. In the process they had suffered 5,296 casualties. During the attempt to eject the Germans from Norway the Allied land force had at no time amounted to more than the equivalent of two and a half divisions, or approximately 24,000 men and of this total the British lost 1,869 and the French and Poles approximately 530. The campaign was the first occasion in the Second World War in which British troops, both Regular and Territorial, had met the Germans in battle, and it had clearly shown the importance of tactical air support, adequate scales of equipment, and appropriate training. The British were not, however, given time to assimilate the lessons of the Norwegian Campaign. Long before it was brought to a close they were fighting for survival in France.

Blitzkrieg

On Friday 10 May 1940, nine months after war had been declared, Germany launched its offensive in the West against the armed forces of France, Britain, Holland, and Belgium. The Allied defence comprised 10 British, 22 Belgian, 10 Dutch, and 94 French Divisions, in all some 3,750,000 men organized in 136 Divisions and supporting units. With 134 Divisions available, the German Army was comparable in formations with the Allies, but its manpower total, at 2,760,000, was almost exactly one million men less. Moreover, German inequality extended to armaments and equipment. Although precise figures are not available, it has been estimated that the Allies could marshal nearly 3,600 tanks and 11,500 artillery pieces against 2,600 German tanks and 7,700 guns. Only in the air were the Germans clearly stronger with some 4,000 aircraft ranged, principally, against 1,000 combat-worthy French planes, together with just over 400 aircraft of the Royal Air Force stationed in France. The Germans planned to compensate for their numerical weakness by speed, and by the employment of the *Schwerpunkt*: the concentration of strength at a decisive point.

The German operational strategy was enshrined in *Fall Gelb* (Operation Yellow), which in its final form deployed three armies for the Campaign. In the north, Army Group B (General von Bock) would advance through Holland into

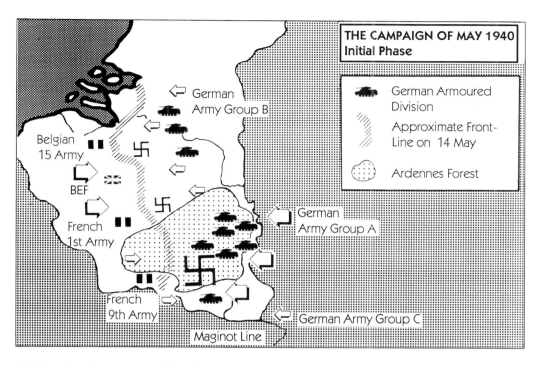

The map labels include:

THE CAMPAIGN OF MAY 1940
Initial Phase

German Armoured Division

Approximate Front-Line on 14 May

Ardennes Forest

German Army Group B

Belgian 15 Army

BEF

French 1st Army

French 9th Army

German Army Group A

German Army Group C

Maginot Line

Belgium drawing as much of the Allied strength as possible to its front. In the south, Army Group C (General von Leeb) faced the Maginot Line from the Swiss border to Luxembourg and would stand on the defensive. In the centre, Army Group A (General von Rundstedt) was responsible for the crucial phase of the German plan. Its task was to burst through the forests of the Ardennes and drive forward between Dinant and Sedan, destroying the centre of the Allied front and cutting their forces in two. Whereas Army Group B comprised twenty-eight divisions, three of them armoured, and Army Group C had seventeen infantry divisions, Army Group A was allocated forty-four divisions, of which seven were armoured.

The French plans for meeting the German offensive were based on a repeat of the opening campaign of the First World War, in which the decisive point of the enemy attack would come in the north, through the Belgian plain. At the first indication of a German attack the Allied Command agreed to advance its troops sixty

miles into Belgium to the River Dyle (Plan D), to form a continuous front from Antwerp to the Maginot Line at Longuyon. Facing the German *Schwerpunkt* in the Ardennes were just nine French infantry divisions. Unlike 1914, the BEF was not to play a significant role in this central struggle for at 1300 hours on 10 May 1940 the British advanced to the north into the path of Army Group B. Next day they took post along the Dyle, east of Brussels, from Louvain to Wavre, and on the afternoon of 14 May they met and held the first German attacks.

The front line was occupied by I Corps (1st, 2nd, and 48th Divisions) and II Corps (3rd and 4th Divisions) with the Belgian Army on their left flank and the French First Army on the right. III Corps (42nd and 44th Divisions) held the line of the River Escaut, while 50th Division took up position on the River Dendre to the west of Brussels, and the 5th Division was placed in support of I Corps. The 'labour' Divisions, 12th, 23rd, and 46th, provided defence against paratroops and saboteurs, and undertook road-

'AGAINST ALL ODDS'

A13 Mk II cruisers of 5th RTR move forward to meet the advancing German panzer divisions in France, 1940
Courtesy of the Tank Museum

control duties.

Although the British successfully repulsed further German attacks, it was obvious by the evening of 15 May that the determining factor in the BEF's fight would be the situation on its flanks. The Dutch Army had already surrendered, and with the position 'fluid' to right and left the BEF pulled back to conform to the movements of the French First Army. I and II Corps retired westwards to the River Dendre and by 19 May had formed a new front with III Corps on the line of the River Escaut. Events to the south were becoming ever more threatening, however, as the armoured spearhead of Army Group A pushed westwards through a disorganized French defence, cutting the BEF's supply line and laying bare its southern flank. A number of composite units, many named after their commanding officers, were formed to strengthen the BEF's right, particularly around Arras. PETREFORCE (Major-General Petre) was ordered to hold Arras, while FRANKFORCE (Major-General Franklyn) defended Vimy. Alongside MACFORCE (Major-General Mason Macfarlane), POLFORCE (Major-General Curtis), WOODFORCE (Colonel J Wood), and other improvised formations, these flank guards

played a vital part in delaying the German advance.

By midnight on 20 May German tanks had reached the Atlantic coast near Abbeville. The Allied front had been cut in two. The difficulty which now presented itself to the German command was how best to exploit this strategic triumph. Should Army Group A swing south-west to trap the French armies against the Maginot Line, press northwards to encircle the Allied armies, or concentrate on securing its flanks which now extended across the breadth of France? Beset by the indecision of the High Command the German Armoured Divisions stood idle throughout 21 May. It was in fact the British who were about to take the initiative.

'Counter-Attack'

The town of Arras was central to the defence of the BEF's southern flank, and it was here that the British were preparing to capitalize upon the initiative which it was hoped their two reserve divisions (5th and 50th) could provide. The operation planned for the afternoon of 21 May, however, stopped short of anything which could be described as a strategic 'counter-attack'. The orders issued, were for an operation by the 5th and 50th Infantry Divisions, plus the 1st Army Tank Brigade, which would support the garrison of Arras by blocking the roads south of the town and interrupting German communications. It was primarily a spoiling attack at a time when even a single hour's delay imposed on the advancing German armour was of crucial importance to the British divisions still fighting to the north. Accordingly, a brigade from each of the two infantry divisions (both of which were under strength with only two brigades instead of three) was despatched to bolster the defences around Arras. With the second brigade (17th) of the 5th Division held in reserve, the initial advance would be carried out by a single Infantry Brigade (151st) of the 50th Division, supported by those tanks of the 1st Army Tank Brigade which remained roadworthy, and a scratch force of artillery and motorcycle troops. French mechanized cavalry was to co-operate on the right flank. Thus the Arras 'counter-attack' was in essence mounted by two battalions of the Durham Light Infantry, with one in reserve, and seventy-four tanks, of which only sixteen mounted ordnance heavier than a machine gun.

Although the attack made progress it was too weak either to exploit its early success, or to hold the ground it had won against German counter-attacks. As night fell, those units still in contact with the enemy withdrew after setting fire to their damaged or broken-down tanks and Bren gun carriers. That for a time the British advance spread alarm, bordering on panic, through the German troops it encountered is indisputable. The 7th *Panzer* Division (Major-General Irwin Rommel), leading the armoured spearhead of Army Group A, lost heavily in men and material and reported that it had been attacked by 'hundreds of enemy tanks and following infantry.' The British attack fulfilled the worst fears of the German High Command, who for days had witnessed their armoured formations surging forward and the infantry struggling to keep in touch. The flanks of the advance were far from secure and the German Command lived in dread of an Allied counter-attack aimed at isolating the spearhead. At Arras they believed it had finally come, and they were badly shaken by the apparent ease with which their front had been penetrated.

With the BEF fighting for its existence in the north, Lord Gort was acutely conscious of the need to re-establish operational contact with the French armies to the south, but he was also aware that the gap in the Allied front could only be repaired by the weight of divisions available to the French. It was beyond the resources of the BEF to close the gap single-handed, yet British divisions would certainly participate in the attempt. This task was assigned to a counter-attack that was planned to take place after the operation at Arras, in which the British would drive south to meet a French offensive northwards. It would not, however, be possible before 26 May, and by then it was abundantly clear that the French Army, worn out by two weeks of hard fighting against the bulk of the German strength, had already dismissed any idea of a counter-attack, and that the ability of the Belgian Army to protect the left of the BEF was coming to an end.

The Channel Ports

With its line of communication to the south cut by Army Group A, the French Channel ports north of the River Somme - Boulogne, Calais, and Dunkirk - became vital arteries for the BEF, both in terms of supply and as possible centres for evacuation. Steps had been taken as early as 22 May to secure these ports with the arrival from England of 20th (Guards) Brigade at Boulogne, and 3rd Royal Tank Regiment (detached from 1st Armoured Division), with 30th Brigade, and a Territorial battalion, the 1st Queen Victoria's Rifles, at Calais. Although these units left England under strength and almost entirely lacking in supporting arms, their arrival in France was timely, for at midday on 22 May the German drive northwards along the Channel coast towards Dunkirk began. The shock administered by the 'counter-attack' at Arras was still apparent within the High Command, however, for the armoured thrust (Guderian's XIX Corps) was weakened by the diversion of units to guard against the possibility of enemy attacks from the south or east. Thus while the 1st

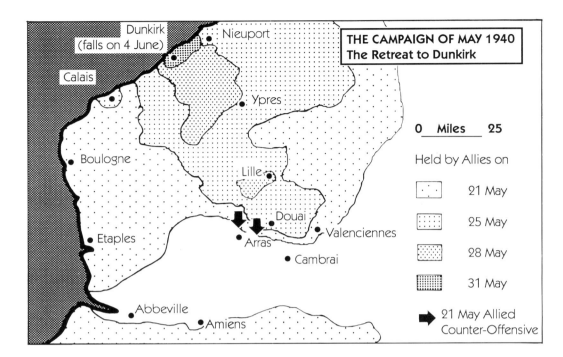

and 2nd *Panzer* Divisions moved on Calais and Boulogne, 10th *Panzer* Division, which should have advanced to Dunkirk, was held in reserve.

The defenders of Boulogne made contact with the German advance during the afternoon of 22 May. The first attacks were repulsed, but the task of holding a six-mile perimeter against an armoured division was beyond the strength of two battalions of the Irish and Welsh Guards. Heavy fighting continued throughout the 23rd, before, as dusk fell, the order was given to evacuate. There followed a remarkable scene as Royal Navy Destroyers fought their way into Boulogne harbour, engaging German tanks, artillery, and machine guns as they successfully embarked all but 300 of the Guardsmen.

By 24 May the garrison of Calais was under heavy attack and its supporting armour had already been reduced to a strength of twenty-one tanks in encounters with the German 1st and 6th *Panzer* Divisions. Pressed-in by enemy infantry and tanks and subjected to massive artillery and aerial bombardment the men of the 1st Rifle Brigade, 2nd King's Royal Rifle Corps, 1st Queen Victoria's Rifles, 3rd Royal Tank Regiment, and 229th Anti-Tank Battery RA, fought doggedly in the streets and from behind the ramparts of Calais. Gradually, as losses mounted and ammunition ran short, the surviving infantry were broken into pockets of resistance which the Germans were able to overcome in turn. Evacuation having been ruled out by the British Government 'for the sake of Allied solidarity', the defenders fought on until they were overwhelmed. Though ending in withdrawal and surrender the British and French defence of Boulogne and Calais had delayed the German advance northwards for nearly four days; time that was vital to the survival of the BEF.

Operation 'Dynamo'

As the last resistance in Calais died, an Admiralty order was sent out from London for the commencement of Operation 'Dynamo', the evacuation of British troops from France.

With the sea at its back, the BEF, virtually surrounded, fought desperately to maintain its flanks as the resistance of the Belgian Army faltered. Dunkirk was the last port in Allied hands offering any hope of successful evacuation, and orders were given for a perimeter defence to be prepared. On 24 May, when the 1st *Panzer* Division had advanced to within fifteen miles of Dunkirk, a remarkable order was given to the German armoured divisions. They were told to halt. By 27 May when the attack resumed, the perimeter defences had been strengthened, and the port of Dunkirk held out until 4 June, by which time most of the BEF had reached Britain. The justification given for the order to halt was that the low-lying ground around Dunkirk was unsuitable for the operation of tanks, that the Armoured Divisions must be preserved for the coming battle in the south, and that the final destruction of the BEF was an appropriate role for the German Air Force (*Luftwaffe*). Certainly, the *Luftwaffe's* eagerness to accept this task came as a relief to many senior officers, who were still anxious about the security of their flanks and the lack of support behind the advance units. Equally, the armoured divisions had suffered substantial losses in both men and equipment, and the troops were extremely

The British Army during the 'Phoney War', as seen by the French magazine *L'Illustration*

tired. A pause while the *Luftwaffe* had its day was not unwelcome. Attempts by the Army High Command to resuscitate the ground advance foundered on the opposition of Hitler and of their own commander (von Rundstedt) of Army Group A.

When the German tanks finally moved forward on the morning of 27 May they encountered an enemy 'fighting tenaciously' and who 'to the last man remain at their posts'. By 30 May the bulk of the BEF's units were within the Dunkirk perimeter and the evacuation was fully underway, with an armada of vessels lifting British, French, and Belgian troops from the harbour and the open beaches. By the afternoon of 4 June when the evacuation officially ended, a total of 338,226 Allied troops had been evacuated. A measure of the success of both the evacuation itself and of the defence of Dunkirk, lies in the fact that 224,320 men of the BEF were saved instead of the 45,000 men it was thought might possibly be got away by sea when 'Dynamo' started. A substantial debt was owed to the French units which provided the final rearguard. Without their willingness to fight on when all seemed lost for their country, the total of Allied troops rescued would inevitably have been reduced. Though battle-hardened soldiers had been saved for the nucleus of the armies that would fight in the Middle East and eventually again in Europe, their weapons and equipment had not. Of the equipment shipped with the BEF, 63,879 vehicles, 20,548 motor cycles, and 2,472 guns had been destroyed in action, or abandoned on the approaches to Dunkirk.

The Battle of France

With the conclusion of Operation 'Dynamo' nearly 140,000 British troops remained in France, south of the Somme. Many were line of communication troops, but there were three fighting formations deployed in the French front line. The 51st (Highland) Division, which had been stationed on the Saar front when the German offensive in the north was launched, had moved west to join the 1st Armoured Division under the command of the French Seventh Army. A further British infantry division had been created from *ad hoc* units - principally BEAUFORCE, DIGFORCE, and VICFORCE - by Brigadier (later Major-General) A B Beauman. The 1st Armoured Division which had only begun to land in France on 15 May, was without its artillery, all its infantry and one regiment of tanks. Its operational strength was 143 cruiser and 114 light tanks.

Both the 51st Division and the 1st Armoured Division mounted spirited attacks against the German bridgeheads over the Somme, notwithstanding their lack of supporting arms.

In the face of the overwhelming offensive launched by the enemy on 5 June, however, the 1st Armoured Division and the bulk of Beauman Division were forced to withdraw across the Seine, leaving the Highlanders north of the river. By 9 June, the 51st Division was effectively cut off from the main Allied force, its only viable course of action being withdrawal to the coast in the hope of evacuation. With German armour already across its line of retreat to Le Havre, the Division withdrew to the small harbour of St Valery en Caux. Although the Royal Navy was waiting off shore, direct German fire into the harbour area, the collapse of French resistance, and a thick blanket of fog rendered evacuation impossible. With the failure of a final counter attack and in response to a clear order from its French superior officer, the 51st (Highland) Division acknowledged the inevitable and laid down its arms.

German soldiers making a propaganda film in the ruined streets of Dunkirk after the evacuation of part of the BEF, June 1940, from the French-language edition of *Signal*

It was clear that the 'Battle of France' was lost, and Lieutenant-General Sir Alan Brooke, sent to assess the position, had no hesitation in ordering the evacuation of the remaining British troops in France. By 18 June the surviving units of the 1st Armoured Division, Beauman Division, and the recently landed 52nd Division (of which only the 157th Brigade had been engaged), had sailed from Cherbourg. The last Allied troops did not leave southern France, however, until 14 August, by which time 191,870 Allied soldiers had been evacuated from ports south of the Somme. The British Expeditionary Force was home at last, but it had suffered 68,111 casualties during the campaign.

In a little under seven weeks, at a cost of 156,000 men killed, wounded, or missing, Germany had conquered Holland, Belgium, and France, and ejected the British from the mainland of Europe. For the German Army, however, the failure to destroy the British Expeditionary Force was a significant setback which was compounded by the subsequent postponement of the invasion of Britain. Even if it was not apparent to the German High Command, the Army knew that a dangerous enemy had been allowed to escape. For in the words of a report prepared by the German IV Corps which had fought the BEF from the start of the campaign:

'The English Soldier was in excellent physical condition. He bore his own wounds with stoical calm. The losses of his own troops he discussed with complete equanimity. He did not complain of hardships. In battle he was tough and dogged. His conviction that England would conquer in the end was unshakeable.'

Members of the BEF as prisoners of war in Stalag XX in 1941
Private collection

Further Reading

Bond, Brian *France and Belgium 1939-1940* London, Davis-Poynter, 1975

Cooper, Matthew *The German Army 1933-1945: Its Political and Military Failure* London, Macdonald and Jane's, 1978

Derry, T K *The Campaign in Norway* London, HMSO, 1952

Ellis, Major L F *The War in France and Flanders 1939-1940* London, HMSO, 1953

Fraser, General Sir David *And We Shall Shock Them: The British Army in the Second World War* London, Hodder and Stoughton, 1983

Kennedy, Major-General Sir John *The Business of War* London, Hutchinson, 1957

Author's Note: Few sources agree on the statistics relating to the campaigns of 1940. Unless otherwise stated the figures given are based on those published in the British Official Histories.

Sunday 3 September 1939 changed the Regular soldier's life. In a matter of hours his priorities passed from those of peacetime to those of war. Most Regulars viewed this transition with a calm professionalism, seeing the outbreak of hostilities as an extension of the job they were paid to do. Colonel P S Newton then an officer cadet at the Royal Military College, Sandhurst, remembered being told to assemble after church parade in his Company ante-room to hear the Prime Minister's radio announcement that Great Britain was at war with Germany: *There was no cheering or anything like that. There was absolute dead silence. We were just nineteen and it was fairly momentous, but the reaction was that we were trained to be soldiers and let's get on with it as soon as possible.*

Call-Up

For the male civilian population that Sunday in September was also a significant date. On that day the National Service (Armed Forces) Act was passed by Parliament and 'all male British subjects between the ages of 18 and 41' became 'liable by Royal Proclamation to be called up for service in the armed forces of the Crown'. For the civilians 'called-up' there was no right to decline military service, unless in holy orders, detained under the Lunacy and Mental Treatment Acts, registered as a blind person, or working in a reserved occupation essential to the war effort. Applicants for the Register of Conscientious Objectors presented their case to local Tribunals, but even where they were included on the Register they could still be called up for service in the Army on non-combatant duties. Everyone subject to

> 66 *And I just said 'Well, I've got to go' and my boss gave me my money up to that day, and we cycled home and got all our kit and gear together and reported to our local HQ, which was the local Parish Hall in my case* 99
>
> Mr Cecil Daniels of 5th Battalion The Buffs , speaking about his mobilization on 2 September 1939

conscription was medically examined and placed in a category which governed their fitness for particular duties. They were also interviewed, and then allocated for enlistment through the Ministry of Labour and National Service which posted non-tradesmen direct to Corps Training Centres. The general principle governing the recruitment of officers was that they should be selected from the ranks and pass through an Officer Cadet Training Unit before receiving a commission.

Training

With the coming of compulsory military service, the first stage of which had been introduced by the Military Training Act on 26 May 1939, the Regular soldiers of the Army were faced with a mass of civilians, totally unused to the routine and rigour of military life, who had to be trained to defend themselves and their country. The scale of the problem can be gauged by the fact that 761,600 men and 31,960 women were taken into the Army as volunteers, conscripts, or as the result of mobilization, between 3 September and 31 December 1939. Not all required training from scratch as the men of the Territorial Army were at least partially trained upon embodiment.

The initial hurdle for the conscript and volunteer alike was a period of fourteen weeks basic training. Most soldiers remember the course consisting principally of drill, weapons training, and route marches. Training in Britain was carried out in something of a vacuum during the Phoney War. Lieutenant Newton, now commissioned from Sandhurst into the

Enlistment notice to Private A A Leach, Royal Army Ordnance Corps 8 November 1940
National Army Museum 7706-73-3

Royal Sussex Regiment, reported for duty at an Infantry Training Centre based at Seaford. He recalled that during his time at Seaford *there was no question of defence; there was no threat of landings; no operational role for the training unit on the beaches of Sussex, and we saw no enemy aircraft.* At Seaford morale during basic training was high and the recruits attitude was that *Hitler was a threat to the peace of the world that had to be eliminated, and everybody accepted that.*

Between September 1939 and May 1940 the men of the BEF spent a great deal of their time training and maintaining their equipment. There was a considerable amount of improvisation and 'making do' required to prepare for battle, for as the Controller of Ordnance Services stated in a report on the mobilization of the BEF: *Hardly a unit went to France completely equipped, and the stocks of technical stores and spare parts were never anything like sufficient either to make good the deficiencies or to maintain the equipment of*

the Expeditionary Force. For the soldier, the days were filled with vehicle maintenance, weapons training, the construction of field defences, and tactical schemes carried out in the surrounding countryside. If the weather made training impossible there were always fatigues to be carried out, unloading stores or cleaning equipment and accoutrements.

With the BEF

For many of those called to the colours in September 1939 their voyage to France with the Expeditionary Force was the first occasion on which they had left the shores of Britain. In the days before mass package holidays, the other ranks, in particular, had not just lacked the opportunity of travelling to France, they had possessed neither the inclination nor the wherewithal to travel anywhere outside the British Isles. Their arrival in Western France thus gave rise to a mixture of emotions typical of an island race encountering what appeared to be a perplexing and alien land for the first time. For Trooper Munns of the 13th/18th Hussars who arrive in Brest on Tuesday 17 September, it seemed *a totally different world altogether.* Billeted in the village of Landerneau, Trooper Munns found that encounters with the local cuisine left a great deal to be desired. *Eggs, but they don't fry them properly. They cook them. Bread, they give you in big chunks. Tea, they cannot make at all, and I didn't like coffee.*

When not in front-line positions the men of the BEF were billeted in French towns or villages, living on many occasions alongside the civilian owners of the houses and barns in which the troops were quartered. The local population was officially declared to be friendly, and the accommodation, though often verging on the rustic, was tolerable for active service. By 3 October 1939 Trooper Munns had arrived at

'The Foot-Slogging Ghost on the old Menin Road', a watercolour by Bruce Bairnsfather, shows the eerie
similarity between 1914 and 1939-40
National Army Museum 8906-73

'AGAINST ALL ODDS'

the village of Ransart and a comfortable billet on a farm: *The madam of the farm has given us the use of the outhouse they use for separating the milk. We have put some straw down in the carrier, and we have a table, and some chairs, so we are not badly off. The only snag is they still separate the milk here morning, and night. Have bought quite a stock of food in and really wouldn't mind this for the duration.*

During the very cold winter months of 1939-1940 the tempo of military life inevitably slackened, and there were opportunities for relaxation. Trooper Munns, now ensconced with seven members of his regiment in a house in Bainey Notre Dame, purchased a dart board, cards, and a radio to fill the long winter evenings in the billet. Saturday 6 January 1940 was a typical winter day: *Half of the Squadron went out on a scheme. I was one of those left behind. Glad really, because I could lay in until 9.00, when I had to go on fatigues. Picking up stores....Nothing in afternoon. Played cards and listened to Everton v Manchester football from Goodison. Had tea in billet but margarine we won from dining hall had petrol in it. Foiled again. Played nap again at night, won about 100F. Wireless still going strong. Good investment.*

Morale

An essential element in the soldier's morale was contact with his home and family. In 1939-40 a soldier going overseas was allowed a period - usually only a matter of days - of embarkation leave before he sailed, but once he was abroad his only regular contact with home was through writing and receiving letters. The importance of 'mail from home' to morale was recognized by the fact that personnel of the Army Postal Service began to move to France on 4 September, the day after war was

declared. Mail collected in England was dispatched from Southampton to Cherbourg, from whence it followed the rations to the front line. Nevertherless, a soldier serving in Armentières could expect to receive a letter posted in Accrington within three to four days. Once a postal route was established between Folkestone and Boulogne in December 1939, the transit time for a letter was further reduced to two or three days. A private telegram could be sent from a Post Office in Britain to a soldier serving with the BEF in even quicker time, and this service was used extensively.

Any mention of military matters in private correspondence was of course forbidden, and normal letters had to be franked by an officer and bear a unit censor stamp before they could be posted. Field Service Post Cards (AFA 2042) were not censored, but they could only be used as a token that all was well with the sender, since the information placed on them was limited to the date, address and the name of the sender. A special Green Envelope (AFA 3078) was provided for communicating private and family matters and this would not normally be opened by the Censor. Private Allan Barratt of the 2nd Survey Regiment, Royal Artillery, while billetted in Normandy in October 1939 found that his unit censor was taking things very seriously: *In my letter home I wrote yesterday, I mentioned the orchard and the tasty apples and pears, but the officer who was censoring the mail called me over and said RHQ had given guidelines on what cannot be mentioned in letters and indication or reference to our whereabouts was taboo, and I'm not allowed to mention the orchard.*

During the Phoney War the Army Postal Service dealt with an avalanche of mail, particularly at Christmas 1939, which included not only letters, but newspapers, food and comfort parcels, postal orders, and vast quantities of souvenirs from France. On many occasions the Army handled more than 9,000 sacks of mail in a single day. Although the German offensive in May 1940 disrupted this network, mail from Britain was being distributed in the area of Dunkirk up to 22 May, and letters were accepted from soldiers for posting home until 29 May, less than a week before the completion of the evacuation from Dunkirk. The crucial importance of this service was caught by an entry in Private Barratt's diary written as his unit was pulling out of Belgium on Saturday 18 May: *And how wonderful, that in all this chaos we had a delivery of mail so that at least some of us are able to forget the war, the bombing, the refugees, if only for a few wonderful moments as we read the letters from our families and friends.*

Other aids to the maintenance of morale included entertainment provided for the troops through mobile cinema units and variety shows. Since it was feared that a mechanized army would not get the exercise it needed, the soldier was also encouraged to take part in sports such as soccer, rugby, baseball, and hockey. Each battalion was allocated eight hundredweight of sports equipment which included twenty-four hockey sticks, fifty pairs of football boots, and clothing sufficient to kit-out six teams.

Into Battle

The fighting in Norway and France in 1940 was, from the British Army's point of view, essentially an infantryman's war. The infantry could not have survived without the support of the other arms in battle, but in terms of immediate and protracted contact with the enemy, it was the foot soldier who bore the brunt. Indeed the local circumstances of battle often dictated that units of supporting arms had to be employed as infantry since they were the only troops available. Thus engineers, heavy and medium artillery, searchlight units, surveyors, cooks, drivers, and clerks, and even on one occasion a mobile bath unit, took up rifles and machine guns to defend themselves at close quarters.

The campaign for the British soldier was characterized by a swift advance to meet the enemy, an abrupt about-face, and a fighting withdrawal, ending in evacuation. All within the brief period of three weeks. This was the more exasperating for in the East the German attacks were generally repulsed and, where ground was lost, it was retaken in local counter-attacks. Private Barratt manning a gunner observation post close to Louvain on 16 May 1940, from where he had watched the Royal Artillery making life extremely unpleasant for the Germans, was stunned by an order to pull out: *Back at the billet I had just thought of a couple of hours kip when we had the biggest shock of our lives. Our OP had had a message from HQ and passed it down to us that we had to pack up, close down the OP, and report to the wagon lines. We could not understand it. Tom Harris up at the OP said he could not see anything unusual happening on the front around Louvain, so surely we are not retreating.* In the West, where the front was lightly held breakthroughs were inevitable, and here British soldiers, many formed into scratch units for local defence, often fought on until they were overwhelmed. It was a war of arrival, encounter, demolition, and departure, in which movement by day, on any scale, drew the swift and deadly attention of the German Air Force. The ferocity and accuracy of the enemy bombing made a lasting impression on the British troops. As Colonel Sir Thomas Butler, serving with the Grenadier Guards, recalled: *Anybody who has*

80

The medal group awarded to Captain J C Crisp, Royal Artillery
1939-45 Star, Africa Star, France and Germany Star, Defence Medal 1939-45, British War Medal 1939-45.
In 1948 the town of Dunkirk issued the bronze medal commemorating the evacuation, and in 1970 the
Dunkirk Veterans Association approved the wearing of the medal
National Army Museum 8905-80

been bombed by a German Stuka doesn't like it. They screamed down with their awful sirens going, bombing, and firing tracer ammunition on the refugees who were flooding the roads. It was a most appalling sight which I shall never forget.

As the retreat continued so the frustration of the BEF grew. Private Barratt and his unit, once again in France, wanted nothing more than a chance to hit back: *I tried several times to tune into the BBC on our little wireless, but no luck...A French announcer said Jerry panzer divisions are pressing on towards the coast, which means we might find ourselves cut off from the French troops in the south. We can't make head or tail of it, and why we have to keep retreating all the time...Some twit is singing 'we'll hang out the washing on the Siegfried Line', but if he doesn't shut up singing that particular song someone will be hanging him out on a line.* For many, withdrawal meant a desperate struggle between approaching exhaustion and the need to keep pace with the shifting tide of battle. After manning a road block outside Ypres for most of the night on Sunday 26 May, Trooper Munns and his comrades withdrew in the face of heavy shell fire. Once out of range he snatched a brief respite in his Bren gun carrier: *I slept in the seat for an hour or two, and at 4.30am we left. We went back to the other side of Ypres,*

and put the vehicles in a shed of a farm. I was so tired I just fell down on some straw and fell dead asleep. Someone was good enough to make a drink of tea, and I was awakened at 8.0am to drink it. I had a wash and a shave then fell asleep again. There were also short, savage encounters with the enemy: *Arrived at a small town about 6.0pm. Was told that in a nearby town about four miles away 'a few Jerry infantry were loose' and we had to round them up. 'B' Squadron were already in there...By the time we arrived at the stopping place, the wounded started coming back. It was a massacre. They immediately stopped our troop from going in, because they found out it had been a mistake. One bloke told me there was at least three or four thousand Jerries there.*

The final days of the withdrawal saw the men of the BEF indulging in an orgy of destruction as they rendered their vehicles and equipment useless before setting out on the march to Dunkirk and evacuation. With a growing sadness Private Barratt and his comrades carried out their orders: *We smashed the vehicles radiators, petrol tanks, distributors and so on, slashed their tyres, smashed the batteries, some engines were driven dry until they seized up Wireless sets also smashed up, everything which may be of use to Jerry.* As they neared the coast the horror that awaited them at Dunkirk became all

'AGAINST ALL ODDS'

too obvious: *It was dusk by the time we reached Dunkirk and we could see the fires blazing fiercely, buildings silhouetted in the red glow, it did look frightening.* Whilst waiting at a road block on the outskirts of Dunkirk, Private Barratt and his comrades heard the sound of tracked vehicles coming towards them out of the night. *Someone feeling panicky was whispering 'sounds like tanks'. When the vehicles neared the road block some stupid clot on guard yelled in a true parade ground manner: 'Halt! who goes there?' And back came the answer very loud and clear 'Adolf xxx Hitler! Who the xxx hell do you think it is!' ...in a lovely broad Scottish accent.*

As the German advance pushed closer to the coast, more and more British soldiers found themselves within the Dunkirk perimeter. Those not involved in rearguard actions were directed to the harbour or the neighbouring beaches to await evacuation by sea. Private Barratt wondered at the audacity of it all: *Towards Dunkirk, the troops could be seen in lines like dark snakes extending down into the sea itself, they appeared to be wading out to small boats some distance out from the water's edge. In front of us too, small boats were picking up men off the beach and taking them out to ships waiting off shore. We gazed at all these hundreds of troops and wondered how on earth we are all going to be lifted out - and there are thousands more yet to come.* Despite intensive bombing and accurate shell-fire the vast majority were saved by the combined efforts of the Royal Navy and the armada of 'small ships' which sailed from Britain. Receptions such as that which awaited Private Barratt at Ramsgate lifted the spirits of the 'beaten' army: *We were led off along the promenade where we boarded buses to take us to the railway station where a make-shift canteen had been set up, with trestle tables piled high with sandwiches and buns*

and mugs of tea, and we were told to 'get stuck-in lads'. We were given bars of chocolate and cigarettes (where from I don't know!). Also handed cards and told to address them to our next-of-kin with some message such as 'Home safely', sign them, and the postcards would be delivered free to our folk at home. How wonderful we thought and how well organised. We were amazed at the reception given to an army which had just been kicked out of France!

Prisoners of War

For the men of the BEF who fought and were taken prisoner, there remained the long journey into captivity in POW camps in Germany and Poland, and the prospect of an indeterminate period of separation from their homes and families. Nearly all were posted as missing and

Many men were taken prisoner in France, and these two sets of identity tags mark the progress of Private Arthur Simister of the Royal Army Ordnance Corps from enlistment to POW camp
National Army Museum 8209-10

in many cases it was to be months before confirmation came via the Red Cross that they were indeed alive and Prisoners of War. Some did not complete their journey and reports reached Britain that they had been summarily killed by the enemy. The men lost in this tragic manner came predominantly from the Royal Norfolk, Cheshire, and Royal Warwickshire Regiments. For most, their passage East began with a long trek out of the battle zone to an appropriate rail-head where they were loaded aboard cattle trucks. In some cases the march presented fleeting opportunities for escape; in others there were encounters with the enemy which brought surprising discoveries. At the beginning of June a British soldier lay exhausted with other POWs at the side of a road in Belgium: *A westbound German horse-drawn battery of field guns also halted. This brought a horse's feet in uncomfortable proximity to my face. Thus I was able to read a partly outgrown hoof brand: 'Innis'. I informed a fellow victim that this was a British Army Horse. In cultured English the officer on the horse remarked 'Yes, it was bought in Ashford market in 1937 and not so much of the 'bloody bastard' if you please.'*

Sources referred to in the Text

The Second World War 1939-45 Army, Mobilization London, The War Office, 1950

Barratt, Allan *My Diaries of events and thoughts 1939-1943* National Army Museum 8908-5

Diary of R W Munns 13th/18th Hussars...Including the Campaign in France 1940 and the withdrawal from Dunkirk National Army Museum 7612-22

Oral history interview with Colonel P S Newton, Royal Military College and Royal Sussex Regiment 1939-40
National Army Museum 8908-116

Oral history interview with Colonel Sir Thomas Butler, Grenadier Guards 1939-40
National Army Museum 8907-68

Daily Telegraph 19 July 1989, letter from M Few

83

.38in No 2 Mk1 Revolver, Serial No A9557, dated 1932
National Army Museum 8204-769-2

'AGAINST ALL ODDS'

CHRONOLOGY

Events directly affecting or involving the British Army. *Political and other events*

1938

September *Munich Crisis - Czechoslovakia demilitarized*

30 September *Chamberlain returns home from Munich promising 'peace for our time'*

1939

22 February British Cabinet decides to equip a field force of four regular infantry divisions, one mobile division, and four territorial divisions to fight on the continent

15 March *German Army occupies Prague*

29 March Hore-Belisha announces doubling of size of the Territorial Army

31 March *Britain and France guarantee Poland against German aggression*

13 April *Guarantees extended to Greece and Rumania in the aftermath of the Italian invasion of Albania*

26 April British Government announces its intention to introduce conscription

21 August Territorial mobilization begins

23 August *Germany and the Soviet Union conclude a non-aggression pact in Moscow*

25 August National Defence Companies called out

31 August Regular and Supplementary Reserves mobilized

1 September *Germany invades Poland* - embodiment of the Territorial Army

3 September *Britain and France declare war on Germany - New Zealand and Australia follow suit*

6 September *South Africa declares war on Germany*

10 September *Canada declares war* - First troops of the BEF land in France

27 September *Warsaw surrenders*

17 October German *Luftwaffe* attacks Scapa Flow

30 November *Soviet Union invades Finland*

6-9 December King George VI visits the front - first British soldier killed whilst serving on the Maginot Line

'AGAINST ALL ODDS'

1940

12 March	*Finland agrees to disadvantageous peace with the Soviet Union in Moscow - British plans to aid the Finns are shelved*
18 March	*Hitler and Mussolini meet in the Brenner Pass - Mussolini agrees to join in the War*
9 April	*Germany invades Denmark and Norway in Operation WESERUBUNG*
14 April	British troops land at Harstad in North Norway
17-18 April	British troops land at Molde and Aandalsnes near Trondheim in Norway
2-3 May	Allied forces meet with reverses in Norway - evacuation of all British troops in central Norway
10 May	Operation SICHELSCHNITT - Germans invade Holland, Belgium, and Luxembourg - Allied troops advance to forward defensive positions - BEF takes up positions on the River Dyle - *Chamberlain resigns and the King asks Churchill to form a government*
14 May	First German attacks on British positions - Holland capitulates - German forces attacking through the Ardennes breach the front held by the French 9th Army
15 May	British troops, with other Allied forces in the north, begin phased retreat
20 May	German *panzers* reach the Channel coast west of Abbeville - Allied troops in the north-east are cut off from their comrades to the south
26 May	British government orders Operation DYNAMO - the evacuation of the Army from Dunkirk
4 June	Germans capture Dunkirk
5 June	*Germans launch advance on Paris*
9 June	Last British and French troops withdraw from Narvik
10 June	*Italy declares war on Britain and France and invades south-eastern France*
12 June	51st Highland Division surrenders at St Valery - evacuation of remaining British troops in France accelerates through Cherbourg, St Malo, and other western ports
14 June	*Paris falls to the Wehrmacht*
21 June	*France surrenders to Germany*

'AGAINST ALL ODDS'

Selected relevant items in the collections of the National Army Museum

Archives

Telegram announcing outbreak of war with Germany, received at HQ Calcutta Presidency from General Staff, Simla 3 Sept 1939
5407-34

War Diary of 325 Anti-Aircraft Company RE Searchlight Battery RA August 1939 - May 1941
6111-181

Orders for and papers relating to the Narvik Campaign of 1940 among the papers of W R P Ridgeway, private secretary to Lord Auchinleck
6305-49-2

Hitler's Last Appeal to Reason German propaganda leaflet 19 July 1940
6311-141-2

Major-General H Williams *A Brief Account of the Divisional Engineers, 1st Armoured Division 1939-40* 1951
6710-5

Printed Pamphlet *Record Book for All Arms, Regular Army at Home* AB 142 (War) 1938
7211-33-2

New Testament issued to the BEF in 1939
7410-161

Journal of Colonel J L Maxwell, Royal Scots Fusiliers, attached Sudan Defence Force 1936-44
7412-30

Regimental papers of the Westminster Dragoons, including material on 22 Armoured Car Company and 102 Officer Cadet Training Unit for the period 1939-42
7503-21

War Diary of 23rd (Northumbrian) Division 10-31 May 1940
7512-132-2

Account of operations of 1st Bn The East Surrey Regiment in World War II : Part 1, France and Belgium in 1940, by Major P G E Hill
7602-11

Diary of R W Munns, 13th/18th Royal Hussars, October 1939 - June 1940, including campaign of May 1940 and evacuation from Dunkirk
7612-22

Muster rolls of thirty-one Yeomanry Regiments on mobilization 3 September 1939, supplied to the Imperial Yeomanry Benevolent Fund in February - March 1940
7612-106

Papers relating to war service of Private A A Leach, RAOC and REME 1940-46, including summons to a medical board, result of same, enlistment notice, service and pay books
7706-73

Documents relating to the military service of W J Munn, including service in Royal Sussex Regiment 1939-42
7706-74-6 to -9

Diary of 2nd Bn The Bedfordshire and Hertfordshire Regiment May-June 1940, with casualty lists and maps
7709-118

The Soldiers English-French Conversation
Book published 1939
7808-33

Diary of the travels and work of a detachment
of 101 (Royal Monmouthshire) Field Coy,
attached to 12th Royal Lancers 10 May - 1
June 1940 - the company was engaged in
destoying bridges during the retreat to
Dunkirk
7910-5

History of 560 Field Coy RE in Flanders May -
June 1940
7912-60-1

War map of Europe published September
1939
8011-53-1

Fifty-one issues of The War Papers reprints of
newspapers reporting important
developments in World War II
8107-15

Two diaries used as press-cutting albums by
Baron M Leijonhufoud, containing newspaper
cuttings from British and European papers of
1939-40
8108-10

Memoirs of A W Woolley, 97 Field Rgt RA,
formerly West Kent Yeomanry, including his
recollections of the Campaign of 1940,
evacuation to Dunkirk, and subsequent coast
defence duties
8203-12

Papers of Major-General J G Halstead, DA
and QMG to I Corps during the retreat to
Dunkirk
8204-793

Pages from the News Chronicle for 30 May
1940
8207-22

Official and unofficial War Diaries of 9th
Lancers, France and Belgium April 1940 - July
1941, including diary kept by Major J R
Macdonell and Captains K J Price and R H S
Wynne 4 May - 16 June 1940, and a folder of
reminiscences of those participating in the
Campaign of 1940
8301-26 to -28

War Diary of 12th Lancers 10 May - 1 June
1940
8301-45

Documents relating to preparation of
Hallamshire Bn York and Lancaster Regiment
for war (microfilm - originals in York and
Lancaster Museum)
8303-36

Papers of General Sir Alan Cunningham,
mostly relating to his commands in East and
North Africa, but incuding diary for Feb - Oct
1940 kept by his ADC while Cunningham was
GOC 66th Division, which was based in the
north of England, and GOC 9th Division,
based in Scotland
8303-104

Photograph of telegram received at Peshawar
stating that war has broken out with Germany
26 Aug 1939 (sic)
8307-51

Daily Express war map of Belgium and
Holland 1940
8401-26-5

'AGAINST ALL ODDS'

Maps of the war in Flanders and Brittany 1940 used by Lord George Scott, 10th Hussars
8403-27

Pocket Notes on Identification of German Units, April 1940 published May 1940
8412-33

Papers of Colonel Roderick Macleod DSO MC, whilst General Ironside's Military Assistant 1939-40, including annotated copy of Ironside's diary for January - March 1940
8502-32

The Times unscaled map of the Franco-German Border 1939
8508-6

Notebook kept by Assistant Embarkation Officer at Dover 27 May - 5 June 1940, listing time of arrival, name of ship, and number of men they held (photocopy)
8509-9

Two sheets from series of German Army Staff maps 1937-39
8511-27

Papers relating to Major A D C Smith, Army Commandos, including early service with The Honourable Artillery Company in 1939, and diary of No 5 Independent Commando April - June 1940, covering operations in Norway
8512-32

Geographers' Map Company map of frontier fortifications between France and Germany c1939
8701-55-23

Service documents of Captain C T Witherby, commissioned into The Royal Tank Regiment

from the Westminster Dragoons 1940, including embodiment notice 1 September 1939
8701-106

War Office regulations relating to officers' uniform 1938-39, including instructions on dress to be worn for the duration of the war, issued 20 September 1939
8701-107-1 to -3

Papers of General Sir Andrew Thorne, GOC London District and Major-General commanding the Brigade of Guards 1938-39, and Commander 48th Division BEF 1939-40
8702-31

Memoirs of the Army service of Colonel N M Dillon 1914-46, much of which he spent in the Royal Tank Corps on the Western Front, in Egypt and India (photocopy)
8703-9

List of holders of various staff appointments in I Corps, 1939 - April 1941, from the papers of Major-General J G Halstead
8706-38

Notebook on artillery techniques and equipment, compiled by Major Kenneth Sidney Smith RA 1934-38
8710-11

Edward George Haynes, *The Last Days of Horsed Cavalry : An Account of Skinner's Horse Between the Wars* (photocopied TS)
8711-55

Reprint of the *Bolton Evening News* for 3 September 1939, reporting outbreak of war with Germany
8908-3

88

Diary of Allan Barratt, 2nd Survey Regiment RA, including his part in the campaign of 1940 and evacuation from Dunkirk
8908-5-1

Photographs

Portrait photographs of King George VI, in Field Marshal's uniform, and Queen Elizabeth 1939
5602-217

Photographs of royal inspections of the ATS
6302-65

Group photograph of senior officers, Staff College c1940
6305-49

Photographs of 14th/20th Hussars in Lucknow 1938
6309-106

Armoured cars of 9th Light Tank Coy RTC in convoy from Deolali to Razmak, photographs collected by Major G E C Newland, 2nd Gurkha Rifles, North-West Frontier Mamirogha Column 1938
6506-81-69

Postcard photographs of the Maginot Line
6510-241

Photographs - by Gale and Polden Ltd - of the Army Catering Corps, including examples of cooking equipment, and views of cookhouses in the field and in barracks c1938-40
6603-185-41 to -49

Photographs of the Royal Tank Corps in India 1937-38
7206-9

Four photograph albums of the Aldershot Tattoos of 1935-38, including massed bands, physical training, exhibits, and spectators
7412-31 to -34

Photograph albums compiled by Major W H J Sale, 3rd County of London Yeomanry (Sharpshooters), Britain 1938-41
7503-63-1 and -2

Photograph albums compiled by Lieutenant-Colonel J L Maxwell, Royal Scots Fusiliers 1933-47, including operations in Palestine 1936, manoeuvres in Lower Atbara 1938, training of NCOs and men in the Sudan, with the Sudan Defence Force 1939
7603-17 to 19

26 British official photographs mounted with newspaper cuttings in the form of a booklet, Home Front 1939-40
7605-31

Photograph album of Fusilier Leonard Whittaker, Lancashire Fusiliers, China 1935-38
7605-68

Photograph of the last mounted parade of Skinner's Horse before mechanization, Rawalpindi Nov 1939
7710-9

Photograph album of 12th Lancers, including service in Egypt and Palestine 1928-36, and in UK 1937-39
7711-159

Album of photographs compiled by an officer attached to the Sherwood Rangers Yeomanry, Palestine 1940
7711-160

Six photograph albums compiled by Colonel G F M Stray MC, 5/14th Punjab Regiment, India c1920-39, including photographs of the Cameron Highlanders in Egypt 1939
7810-9 to -14

10 photographs of the last Proclamation parade of Corps of Guides Cavalry and Infantry, Mardan 1939
7810-70

Photograph of men of the Rifle Brigade training with the Boys .55 anti-tank rifle c1938
7905-6-10

Photograph of the Indian Army General Staff in Army HQ, Delhi March 1939
7905-61

Mounted officers and NCOs, 5th Dragoon Guards, in Service Dress, with standards c1938
7906-181

King George VI visiting the Front Line in France, December 1939, visiting the ATS with Queen Elizabeth, and inspecting other British troops 1939-40
8001-8

Photograph of officer group including King George VI and Major-General H R L G Alexander 1939
8204-792-5

Photograph album, 9th Lancers at the Tidworth Tattoos of 1934 and 1936
8401-88 and 90

Photograph album, Royal Tank Corps at the Tidworth Tattoo of 1938
8401-92

Photographs of No 5 Independent Commando 1940, including operations in Norway, collected by Major A D C Smith, Army Commando
8407-16

Postcard photographs of the Gordon Highlanders, Home Front c1940
8407-91

Photographs collected by Colonel Roderick Macleod, Military Assistant to General Ironside: German Army manoeuvres 1937, inspections by Dukes of Windsor and Gloucester, Hore-Belisha, and others of the BEF in France 1939-40, and portrait photographs of Ironside, Deverell, Ribbentrop, Blomberg, Hitler, Goering, Mussolini, Badoglio, and staff officers
8504-49

Sound

78rpm records of military music recorded and published in 1939-40 by Bands of The Grenadier Guards, The Coldstream Guards, The Welsh Guards, The Royal Marines, and German bands of the 1930s - Recordings of Aldershot and Tidworth tattoos of the 1930s, including the Aldershot Tattoo of 1939.
8110-34

Oral history recording by Lieutenant-Colonel Robin Schlaefli, 11th Sikh Regiment, detailing his military experiences in 1939-40
8905-162

Oral history recording by Mr C E Daniels, The Buffs, recalling training with the Territorial Army, and mobilization in September 1939
8905-165

Oral history recording by Colonel Sir Thomas Butler, Grenadier Guards, recounting his experiences with the BEF and his evacuation from Cherbourg in June 1940
8907-68

Oral history recordings by In-Pensioners Alan Moxon and Bert Bowers of the Royal Hospital, Chelsea, recalling the first days of World War II
8907-72

Oral history recording by Sergeant Douglas Young, Royal Corps of Signals, covering his enlistment in 1938, training in Catterick, and service in North Africa 1939-44
8908-111

Oral history recordings by Major V G Matthews recalling his service in both World Wars with the 5th Royal Inniskilling Dragoon Guards and The Leicestershire Regiment
8908-114

Oral history recording by Colonel P S Newton, recounting his memories of service with 5th Bn The Royal Sussex Regiment in the early years of World War II
8908-116

Oral history recording by Brigadier E G Davies-Scourfield, King's Royal Rifle Corps, recalling the battle for Calais, May 1940
8908-143

Oral history recordings made by Westwood Sound Productions to provide material for their series *Images of War* and relating to the first year of war
8908-151

Oral history recording by Sir Basil Hall, detailing his service with the 12th Royal Lancers in Belgium and France May - June 1940
8909-67

Film

Film taken by J P N Graham, Central India Horse, of 17th/21st Lancers in tanks 1938, 3rd Indian Cavalry mechanization course, Ahmednagar June-September 1939
8009-1

The Nazis Strike - Videotape of US propaganda film directed by Frank Capra covering the first year of war - *After the Battle* Series, 1983
8308-23

Extracts from MoI film *A Nation Springs to Arms* (cJan 1940), showing conscription, outbreak of war, embarkation of the BEF, and British troops in France
8907-76

Fine and Decorative Art

'Uniforms of the Territorial Army'
Album of cigarette cards, published by John Player
UR

'Military Uniforms of the British Empire Overseas'
Album of cigarette cards, published by John Player
6112-411

'Defend Britain. Join the anti-aircraft units of
the TA'
Recruiting poster for the Welwyn anti-aircraft
battery
TA Poster No 5 by Lance Cattermole 1938
8108-54

'Safeguard Your Liberties/Join the TA'.
A soldier standing guard across a map of
Britain
TA Poster No 6 by Lance Cattermole 1938
8401-54

'Join the TA anti-aircraft units of the TA'
TA Poster No 3 by Lance Cattermole 1938
8401-55

Searchlight used in TA poster (8401-55)
Pencil drawing by Lance Cattermole 1938
8401-56

Sgt Percy Stanford, 5th Sussex (Worthing) Bn,
Home Guard 1940
Oil on canvas, by Lance Cattermole
8403-54

1st Battalion Grenadier Guards
Six pencil drawings by Lance Cattermole
1938-40
8403-57

'Military Uniforms of the British Empire
Overseas'
Ten single figures in uniforms of Indian Army
regiments and Indian States Forces units
Ten pencil drawings by Lance Cattermole
1937
8403-58

'Military Uniforms of the British Empire
Overseas'
Eleven single figures of regiments from Africa,
Malaya, Mauritius, Singapore, British
Honduras, and Barbados

Eleven pencil drawings by Lance Cattermole
1937
8403-59

Despatch Rider, Royal Signals during the
evacuation of Dunkirk 1940
Oil on canvas by A R Thomson
8506-1

'Back Them Up'
War Office Poster 1940
8511-56

'Scotland For Ever'
TA Poster No 7 by Lance Cattermole 1938
8805-29

'The Foot-Slogging Ghost on the old Menin
Road'
Watercolour en grisaille by Bruce Bairnsfather
8906-73

Weapons

2.5-inch Discharger Cup and No 36 grenade
fitted with baseplate
7608-15-9

Short Magazine Lee Enfield Rifle Mk 3 .303
calibre
8207-81-7

Bren Gun Mk I
6405-60-11

Pistol, Revolver, No 2 Mk I .38 calibre
7811-40

Boys Anti-Tank Rifle .55 calibre
8908-147

Signal Pistol No 1 Mk III
7811-44

Mortar, 3-inch Mk IV
7811-79

Mortar, 2-inch Mk VII
7811-81

Bayonet No 1
8305-98-1

Vickers Mk I Machine-Gun with anti-aircraft
mounting
8905-210

Equipment

Prismatic Compass owned by Lt F M Taylor,
Lancashire Fusiliers1940
7911-35-1

Canvas bowl, bath, and chair, owned by
Captain A White, North Staffordshire
Regiment 1940-45
7408-30

Drawing instruments and cased binoculars
owned by Lieutenant A Sweetenham, Royal
Engineers c1925-40
7701-24

Respirator No 4 Mk II 1939, with case 1940
8205107-1

Map Case owned by Captain N Dawnay,
Lincolnshire Regiment 1940
6407-106-14

Asbestos fire cloak and blanket 1940
6404-23

Toolkit, rifle cleaning 1940
7506-60-3

First Field Dressing 1939
8004-8

Telephone, telegraphy, set Mk V 1940
8106-69

Canteen owned by Captain N Dawnay,
Lincolnshire Regiment 1940
6407-106-14

Bags, holdhall, messtins, blanco, and
'housewife' 1940-45
8105-70

'V' brand cigarettes and matches 1940
8210-4; 8211-175

Uniform

REGULAR FORCES

British Battledress Trousers
7810-35-3

British Battledress Blouse
8607-30-1

Small packs
6407-104

Anklets
7408-16

Ammunition pouches
7406-22/23

Waterbottle carrier
7807-92

Pack straps
7807-93

93

IMPERIAL AND COLONIAL FORCES

Princess Patricia's Canadian Light Infantry 1942
Major's full dress tunic
5301-1

Ceylon Planters Rifles Corps 1940
Captain C C Hope: Cap, boots, lanyard,
overalls
6002-107

Shanghai Light Horse 1939
Corporal E Toeg: NCO cape
8008-28

Singapore Volunteer Corps (Scottish Troop)
1930-35
Doublet, Kilmarnock, Puttees, Socks,
Waistbelt
6404-101

Royal Durban Light Infantry 1935
HRH The Duke of Connaught: Full dress
uniform
6609-18

10th Queen Victoria's Own Corps of Guides
1928-35
Full dress uniform
5101-50; 5910-29-3; 5310-7; 6212-41-5;
6703-3-5

4th Gurkha Rifles 1936
Full dress uniform
6808-28; 5703-18

Medals

1939-45 Star, Africa Star, France and Germany
Star, Defence Medal 1939-45, Medal
commemorating Dunkirk, awarded to Captain J
C Crisp RA. Associated archives, including

notebook on artillery
8905-80

Distinguished Conduct Medal 1918, 1914-15
Star, British War Medal 1914-20, Allied
Victory Medal 1914-19, 1939-45 Star, British
War Medal 1939-45, Long Service and Good
Conduct Medal 1920. Awarded to Lieutenant
A G Dorrington Royal Engineers and Royal
Signals, believed to have died of wounds
received at Dunkirk Associated documents of
service in both wars, and photograph
8905-190

OBE 1946, Order of St. John 1945 and 1950,
1914-15 Star, British War Medal 1914-20,
Allied Victory Medal 1914-20, Defence
Medal 1939-45, British War Medal 1939-45,
Coronation Medal 1953, Efficiency
Decoration 1943. Awarded to Lieutenant-
Colonel A J MacPhail, South Lancashire
Regiment, from 1939 served in Military
Intelligence. Associated documents of service
in both wars, and photograph 8903-4

Distinguished Conduct Medal awarded to
Sergeant J S Huskisson, Royal Engineers, May
1940. On 18 and 19 May Sergeant
Huskisson's Company was engaged in
destroying bridges in the face of the
advancing enemy. A charge failed and
Huskisson went back, reset it, and
successfully blew the bridge
8909-47

95

'AGAINST ALL ODDS'